Greek Islands
of the Aegean

Text Lindsay Bennett
Editorial Erica Spaberg Keirstead
Principal Photographer Pete Bennett
Cover Photography Corrie Wingate
Art Direction Klaus Geisler
Managing Editor Tony Halliday

Berlitz® POCKET GUIDE
Greek Islands
of the Aegean

Sixth Edition 2003

Photography by: Pete Bennett/APA except on pages 3 (top right), 6, 24, 48, 51, 75, 80, 92 by Gregory Wrona/APA; 13 by Bill Wassman/APA; 22 Topham Picturepoint; 61 by David Beatty; 3 (bottom left), 67 and 94 by Phil Wood/APA; 71, 79 and 90 by Terry Harris/Just Greece.

CONTACTING THE EDITORS

Every effort has been made to provide accurate information in this publication, but changes are inevitable. The publisher cannot be responsible for any resulting loss, inconvenience or injury. We would appreciate it if readers would call our attention to any errors or outdated information by contacting Berlitz Publishing, PO Box 7910, London SE1 1WE, England. Fax: (44) 20 7403 0290; e-mail: berlitz@apaguide.co.uk www.berlitzpublishing.com

Chic Mykonos (page 28) is a good option for those in search of a glamorous holiday destination .

For exceptional archeological sites visit uninhabited Delos (page 31).

The unfinished Temple of Apollo is on Naxos (page 42), the largest island in the Cyclades.

TOP TEN ATTRACTIONS

Patmos (page 55) is home to many Byzantine treasures.

▼

Chios (Hios, page 66) has hidden gems, from well-preserved medieval villages to the sheltered Monastery of Nea Moni.

◄

There are few more breath-taking sites in the Aegean than the coloured domes and bell-towers of Santorini.

►

On Skiathos (page 75) you can visit Koukounariès, one of the most stunning beaches in the Aegean.

▼

The best olive oil in Greece is produced on Lesvos (page 62).

►

Paros (page 39) offers fishing ports, archeological sites, traditional white villages and lovely beaches.

►

Although the sponge industry on mountainous Kalymnos (page 58) has waned, tourism is now big news.

►

CONTENTS

Fact Sheets

INTRODUCTION

The classical gods made their home here, fighting their battles, having love affairs, and giving birth to their children. The Persians coveted the islands over 7,000 years ago, and they were stepping-stones on the long east–west trading routes during Hellenistic and Roman times. Throughout most of the last two millennia, they were fought over by European superpowers and became pawns in the religious conflicts between Christianity and Islam. Although they now form part of the modern state of Greece, a deep imprint of history's footsteps can be seen clearly on every dusty hill, in each olive grove and along every coastline. Nowadays, with their hot summer days, warm waters, abundant beaches and distinct lifestyle, the Greek islands of the Aegean are among the major tourist playgrounds in the world.

> The Aegean is just a finger of water 640 km (397 miles) long and 320 km (198 miles) wide, pointing up from the east Mediterranean between Greece and Turkey. It has more than 1,400 islands which, although scattered, form a series of groups each with their own character.

The most accessible islands from Athens are the Cyclades to the southeast, thrown like a handful of pebbles into the sea. In ancient times, they sat in a circle *(cyclos)* around the sacred island of Delos, and their name has carried through into modern times. The islands' barren landscapes and stark white, cube-shaped houses – their blue-shuttered windows bedecked with geraniums – represent the Greek islands to many. The most popular and best known are the lively island

A windmill stands atop a white village on Santorini (Thira).

of Mykonos and the awe-inspiring caldera of Santorini. Collected together in the southeastern reaches of the Aegean Sea are the Dodecanese islands, which rest against the southwest corner of the Turkish coastline. The major island in the group is Rhodes (covered in its own *Pocket Guide*), although Kos and Patmos are also in this group. In the eastern Aegean three of its larger islands mirror the western Turkish coastline: Lesvos, Chios and Samos still have many vestiges of the traditional rural lifestyle that made them rich and coveted in previous centuries.

In the northern Aegean are three more disparate islands – Thassos, Limnos and Samothraki – while southwest of these, closer to Athens, are the Sporades islands of Skiathos, Skopelos, Alonissos, and Skyros (until recently the exclusive playground of the Greek jet set).

The volatile and fascinating history of the whole area means that no two islands are identical, although similarities

What's in a Name?

There are no hard and fast rules governing the Roman transliterations of Greek place names on maps and road signs. Indeed, you will often find the same village name spelled differently on two consecutive road signs. Some names, such as Chios and Hios, are easily recognised as interchangeable, but others can be confusing.

This guide uses the spellings that are generally accepted in Western Europe, but you will find variations, since the Greek alphabet does not directly match the Roman alphabet.

The islands sometimes shun Western names. Santorini is Italian for Saint Irene, the name given to the island in Byzantine times when the saint is believed to have died there. The island's ancient (and official) name is Thira, which is used by airlines and ferry companies on their tickets and printed schedules.

do exist. Despite countless different landlords, the basic way of life for ordinary people has changed little over 5,000 years. The seas produced abundant food for the earliest settlers, and the warm summers brought forth crops of grain that sustained the population and provided grazing for herds of goats from the fifth century BC onwards.

Since the Bronze Age, donkeys and mules have provided a means of transport; around the same time, the first olives and vines were planted here. Life was governed by seasons of sowing, tending and harvesting. Look around the islands

Donkeys have been used for transport since the Bronze Age.

today and there is little cause to think that much has changed.

Tradition plays a great part in island lifestyle. Men and women still lead very separate lives – women are typically based in the home, chatting across balconies festooned with washing or sitting on shady corners, while the men work in the fields or at their boats; older men frequent the *kafeneion* (café) where the world is put to rights over a strong *café ellenikos*.

The family is the core of daily life. Children, especially boys, are seen as a blessing and are treated with indulgence, fussed over by mothers and grandmothers. Grandparents and fathers push the prams of the new arrivals during the evening *volta*, or promenade, glowing in the congratulations of their neighbours and friends. Fathers and uncles employ sons and nephews before any outsider in family businesses.

The siesta remains an important part of the day, with everyone from the youngest to the oldest family member resting during the heat of the afternoon and making the most of the cool evenings, often not going to bed until well after midnight.

Historically, the fabric of life has been sustained by religion. Indeed, the church, and the Orthodox religion, was identified with all that was Greek long before the modern state was created in 1832. Through natural disaster, war and disease, the church has provided a place of refuge and solace, both physically and spiritually. To this day, the priest has a strong influence within the community. Women have traditionally formed the majority of the congregation, praying for the protection of their menfolk while the last were at sea in merchant ships, diving for sponges, or working in distant lands. The smallest whitewashed churches house a simple cross, icon and lit candles, although you will find the largest churches are somewhat more lavish and ornate.

Greece once had the largest merchant fleet in the world, and the sea still plays a major role in the life of the Aegean. On smaller, more remote islands, ferries form the only transportation link with the outside world. They carry essential goods, just as they have done throughout history. Each island has a flotilla of small craft setting sail daily to bring a fresh catch to the tables.

However, tourism has begun to alter this long-standing scenario and is now the biggest money earner in the islands This has saved many islands from the brink of poverty and depopulation, although it is undoubtedly affecting the character of the more popular destinations. Island society has seen more change in the last 20 years than in the previous 1,000. Today, motor scooters drown out the sound of playing children, and mobile phones are heard more frequently than

Ormos, one of the idyllic beaches on Mykonos.

the haunting cadences of the *bazouki*. The harried man walking briskly along the street while taking his call, arm waving in animated fashion, probably has a business empire of restaurants, car-hire agencies, ticket offices and holiday apartments to manage. He needs to keep his finger on the pulse during the short tourist season. As incomes rise, the young farmer buys a truck to replace his father's trusty donkey, or he gives up farming to open a bar. The fisherman uses his boat to ferry tourists to beaches rather than to catch fish.

But all is not lost. Tourism, too, is a seasonal industry, fitting neatly into the traditional cyclical pattern of island life. In spring, before the tourists arrive, goats and sheep give birth, and their herds head out to the open pasture; a little later, the grain crop is harvested. As autumn approaches, another harvest begins: olives, walnuts and almonds must all be gathered and preserved before the start of winter. So, in a sense, island life continues just as it always has.

A BRIEF HISTORY

Prehistoric man in Asia Minor (now modern Turkey) or Greece could look out across the Aegean towards the horizon and see the faint silhouette of land. Their curiosity pushed them to build vessels that were strong enough to ford the open seas and reach these islands, marking the start of the long legacy of Mediterranean seafaring.

Around 7000 BC, the Phoenicians set out from what is now Iran to explore their surroundings. They eventually reached the islands and founded colonies on those in the northernmost part of the Aegean Sea. An important early material, obsidian, was discovered on the island of Milos. Obsidian is a hard, vitreous volcanic rock, which could be fashioned into tools for cutting and stabbing. The high quality of the seam on Milos ensured that the area remained popular with early travellers.

> On geologist's paradise Milos vast quarries disfigure the landscape. Obsidian used to be mined here but bentonite, perlite, barite and china clay are now more common.

The basic elements of life in the Aegean began to come together as early as 5000 BC, and were already in place by the late Bronze Age (c.2700 BC). The major changes were not to daily tasks and routines, but to the political power base, which changed regularly and not necessarily peacefully.

Cycladic Culture

Around 3500 BC, a sophisticated culture evolved in the Cyclades islands. The distinctive, sculpted marble figures of the era are now being reproduced in vast quantities as souvenirs. You will find original examples in the archaeological museums throughout the Cyclades; one of the earliest examples is in the museum on Paros. The people farmed and fished; on the dawning of the Bronze Age in 2700 BC, they began to work with metals. The Cycladic culture was influenced by eastern societies, importing the pottery wheel from Mesopotamia. They also traded in obsidian and local marble.

The Minoans and the Myceneans

Further south in Crete, the Minoan culture developed after 2000 BC into the most significant of its age, spreading its influence throughout the region by trade and diplomacy. Santorini (Thira), the next major

A small statue with arms crossed is typical of early Cycladic culture.

island north, was heavily influenced by Crete, and the settlements of Thira and Akrotiri thrived at this time. The magnificent frescoes and mosaics found at Akrotiri are in Athens at present, but the remains of the buildings at the site provide ample evidence of the sophistication of the culture here.

Around 1500 BC, a massive volcanic eruption at Santorini destroyed not only Akrotiri, but the whole Minoan civilisation. Massive tidal waves swept over Crete, and other parts of the Mediterranean, smashing buildings and drowning many thousands of people. In the wake of this tremendous natural upheaval, the Aegean Islands next came under the influence of the Myceneans (around 1300 BC), who had a

Detail of a mosaic on Delos from the Greek classical period.

base in the Peloponnese on the Greek mainland. The Mycenaeans were an acquisitive race who came to conquer, not to trade. Their extensive military campaigns were later chronicled by Homer in his epic poems *The Odyssey* and *The Iliad*.

The Rise of Athens

The Dorians, from northern Europe, conquered the Mycenaeans. They were a barbaric race, and their custody of the area brought about a dark period during which the written word was forgotten and art disappeared. They held sway over islands off the northern Greek coast, but the Phoenicians kept control of the main sea routes; south of the area, trade continued as usual. At the same time, city-states began to grow in influence on the southern Greek mainland. Athens became the most powerful, heralding the start of the Greek classical period. However, Greece was not yet a country; each city-state was self-governing and autonomous.

The new culture spread throughout the Mediterranean, helped by a huge increase in migration from the mainland to settlements such as Carthage, a Greek city on the African coast of the Mediterranean. Culture and the arts flourished once again. Athletic prowess was admired and the Olympic games were constituted in 776 BC to promote friendly competition. Homer wrote his epic works on Chios and lyrical poetry was much admired, particularly the work of the poets Archilochos on Paros and Sappho on Lesvos.

The pre-eminent islands of this era were Delos, a sacred place and centre of religion ruled by Athens; Samos, ruled by the tyrant Polycrates; and Naxos, whose ruler Lygdamis undertook some major building projects. Archaeology shows that during this time societies lived mainly in coastal towns.

The Persian Wars

As Athens rose in influence and power in the west, it was matched in the east by the rise of the Persian Empire. From a power base in Anatolia, the Persians overran the eastern Aegean Islands and set their sights on the Cyclades. In 490 BC, they captured sacred Delos and razed the settlements on Naxos. The island communities were undecided about which side to back. Paros and Andros contributed to the Persian armoury, while others supported Athens. The two superpowers finally clashed at the epic battles of Marathon and Salamis in 480 BC. The Persians were defeated, and Athens duly punished the islands that had turned against it.

Following its victory, Athens introduced a mutual protection alliance (a NATO of the ancient world). Several islands

---

Homer's Works: One Author or Several?

It is not known whether the works of Homer are the creation of one man or, rather, written versions by several scribes of orally transmitted epics of the eastern Mediterranean. Scholars who believe that two or more writers produced works attributed to Homer think that the *Iliad* was written down by a poet from Anatolia (possibly from Smyrna, now known as Izmir) while the *Odyssey* was recorded by a writer from Chios.

and Greek city-states agreed to work together and, to fund their plans, created a treasury, which was held on Delos. The alliance became known as the Delian League. The league controlled the Aegean and the greater Athenian Empire for most of the fifth century BC. Later, in 454 BC, the treasury was transferred to Athens and its deposits were used to finance the construction of many of the major buildings and temples of the Classical Age.

In 431 BC, Athens began a war with its neighbour and league member Sparta. Although the islands witnessed little action, as the war went on they could see that Athens was slowly losing its power. Before the end of hostilities in 401 BC, many islands had already transferred their allegiance to the victors, who were led by Philip II of Macedon. He was followed in 336 BC by his son Alexander the Great, whose rise to power ushered in the Hellenistic period.

Hellenistic and Roman Periods

When Alexander went on to conquer lands as far to the east as India, the Aegean became a crossroads on the trading routes and Delos was one of the largest marketplaces in the empire. After Alexander's death, much of the Aegean came under the rule of the Ptolemies, along with Egypt. Cleopatra was a member of this famous ruling clan.

Although in 88 BC, Mithradates made a swift and successful raid from the east, the next major power change brought influence from the west. The Greek Hellenistic Empire was gradually, and peacefully, absorbed into the Roman Empire.

The Byzantine Empire and the Coming of Christianity

The Romans ruled a pagan empire, but the Aegean had an important influence on the early development of Christianity. In AD 95, St John arrived on Patmos, a small rocky island in

The monastery on Patmos where St John was imprisoned.

the Dodecanese, as a political prisoner. It was here that he wrote what was to become the final book of the New Testament, *Revelation*. But it wasn't until 330, when the newly converted Emperor Constantine made Byzantium, renamed Constantinople, capital of his Eastern Empire that Christianity was assured of its dominant role in Greek life.

The Byzantine Empire had powerful and well-fortified cities, but the countryside and outlying islands were ravaged by waves of invaders. In an attempt to counter a threat from the Saracen Muslims, a potent religious force from the east, the Byzantine army forcefully enlisted the men of the islands. Disease also took its toll, and, by the time of the Crusades, many of the Aegean islands were almost depopulated.

As the Byzantine Empire weakened at the end of the first millennium, Crusader forces were sent from Western Europe to counter the Muslim forces and retake Jerusalem for the Christian faith. Unfortunately, their zeal was not matched by

An icon adorns the Chapel of the Virgin in the church on Patmos.

their discrimination. The crusaders swept through Byzantium killing Christians as well as Muslims, civilians as well as soldiers. Constantinople was taken by Crusader forces in 1204, and they stripped the city of its finest treasures – many of which now grace the public buildings of Venice. A large consignment of books and manuscripts was transferred to the monastery at Patmos before the city fell.

While Byzantine land was being divided, no one was in control of the seas, so pirates raided towns on many of the islands. To counter this, the populations built settlements inland, out of sight of the raiding parties. This created a pattern seen today throughout the Aegean of a small port *(skala)* which serves an inland settlement *(chora)*, making it easier to resist attack.

The minor Aegean Islands were taken by various powerful European noblemen, many of whom were Genoese or Venetian, such as Marco Sanudo on Naxos. The noblemen had free rein to create their own fiefdoms. The Venetians fortified their main towns – Naxos Town and Antiparos Town are examples – creating labyrinths of narrow alleys and cul-de-sacs that were designed to confuse invaders.

The Genoese took control of the eastern Aegean Islands, which were considered the most valuable for agriculture and trade. After a final bloody defeat by the Muslims in 1309, Christian forces were forced from the Holy Land. The Knights of St John, a holy military force, made their way to Rhodes and Kos in the Dodecanese. They began the process of building their citadels and reinforcing Christianity on the islands. However, they had not seen the last of their Muslim foe. A threatening force was gaining strength in the east.

The Coming of the Ottoman Turks
The Ottomans were roving invaders who came from the east, taking land in what is now Turkey. By the end of the 13th century, they began their first raids on the Aegean Islands. In 1453, they took Constantinople and immediately made it their capital, renaming it Istanbul.

They then set their sights on the islands of the Knights of St John and finally ejected the knights from the Dodecanese in 1522. In 1566, they wrested Chios from the Genoese, bolstering their hold on the eastern Aegean Islands, but the Cyclades remained in Venetian hands for another generation or more – Tinos was the last to fall in 1715. The Ottomans brought new influences to the islands, forming a large empire that stretched around the eastern Mediterranean.

Towards Greek Independence
However, a movement was growing on the Greek peninsula for an independent Greek state. In 1770, Russia, a fellow Orthodox country, came to the aid of the Greeks, declaring war on the Ottoman Empire and occupying several Aegean islands until 1774. Graffiti written by Russian soldiers can be seen in the caves of Antiparos. Although this attempt was unsuccessful, the campaign for a Greek state continued into the 19th century and gathered momentum. The Aegean islands played their part. Lesvos, Chios and Samos lay in the important shipping lanes, and patriots began disrupting Ottoman

cargo traffic. In return, the Turks violently put down every insurrection, including massacring 22,000 people on Chios.

The Ottoman Empire was weakening, and in 1821 the Greek mainland, the Cyclades and the Sporades finally achieved nationhood. A sense of identity enveloped Greeks throughout the Aegean, thus commencing a movement to expand Greece and unify the disparate Orthodox populations.

The 20th Century and Beyond

A series of disastrous decisions at the beginning of the 20th century began to sound a death knell for the Ottoman Empire. The Turks lost a war with Italy, and were forced to relinquish the Dodecanese islands to the Italians. Greece took this opportunity to absorb the islands of the northern and eastern Aegean and to add Macedonia to its mainland territories. The Ottomans then allied themselves to Germany in World War I, losing more territory with the subsequent defeat of Germany. Greece was handed a strip of land along the western coast of Asia Minor, which for more than 2,000 years had had a substantial Greek population. Greece moved in to administer the land, but a new influence upset any dreams of making this region a part of greater Greece.

> **The Aegean islands played an important role in the Greeks' struggle against four centuries of Turkish domination, as the islands' fearless marines put their seafaring talents towards the nationalist cause.**

In 1923, Turkey broke away from the tired Ottoman rulers, and Kemal Ataturk rose to power on a wave of popular support. He promised a modern state for his people, but as the situation became volatile, civil strife broke out in Turkish cities, and those people considered Greek were victims of threats and violence. Thousands had to leave their birthplaces, fleeing to Lesvos, Chios and Samos, the Greek-ruled islands located just offshore. Finally, Greece was ousted from its territory in Asia Minor, which became part of the new Turkish state.

Greece attempted to stay out of World War II, but Mussolini saw Greece as an ideal addition to his Italian empire. His forces made a series of attacks from their

Samos, once the scene of bitter fighting, is now a holiday island.

bases in the Dodecanese islands, including sinking a Greek naval vessel in the harbour of Tinos Town, but they only succeeded in strengthening the resolve of the population against them. Later the Germans came in force and occupied many of the islands.

After the war, in 1947, the Dodecanese islands finally became part of the Greek nation. But the country was politically fragmented, with arguments between monarchists and republicans, right and left, and tension escalated into civil war. The struggle bypassed most of the islands, although there was fierce fighting on Samos. Even after the fighting stopped more than a decade later, the country was not stable.

At the same time, the growth in air and road transport saw shipping decline in importance. The Aegean islands, which for centuries had been important ports on the trading routes, became the backwaters of this new transport network and the economies of several islands came close to collapse.

In 1967, the military took the reins of power in Athens, and until 1974 the 'Colonels' held sway with a repressive and brutal regime. Many Greek islanders chose to leave rather than live in poverty and terror, and made new homes in the United States and Australia. The expansion of air travel heralded the age of mass tourism, and Greece and the Aegean islands became exciting destinations for northern Europeans escaping their damp, cool summers.

In 1982, Greece joined the European Common Market (now the European Union). Since this time, membership has been of great monetary benefit to the country. The EU has given large subsidies to develop Greece's infrastructure and grants to excavate and protect its ancient monuments.

Airfields have been constructed on a number of the islands, and road systems have been expanded and improved. Private investment has even made an increasingly modern ferry and hydrofoil fleet possible.

Politically, the end of the 20th century was a relatively quiet time for the islands, although the divorce of Greek prime minister Andreas Papandreou (died 1996) and his subsequent marriage to a much younger woman caused consternation within conservative Greek society. As the Balkans flared to war once again, Greek nationalism stirred,

The Greek prime minister, Andréas Papandréou, in 1968.

and there have been discussions in the *kafeneion* about the land of Macedonia returning to the fold of its forefathers. Whether this will ever happen still remains to be seen, but perhaps the aid offered by Greece to Turkey after a devastating earthquake in 1999 is a sign that the long-lived animosity between these two traditional enemies is finally beginning to diminish.

Historical Landmarks

7000 BC Phoenicians explore the Aegean.

2000 BC Minoan culture dominates the Aegean.

1500 BC The volcano on Santorini erupts; end of Minoan civilisation.

1450 BC The Mycenaean culture becomes dominant.

1100–750 BC Dorian invasion brings a dark period to the Aegean.

500 BC Persian forces overrun many Aegean islands, until they are defeated by the Athenians in 480 BC.

477 BC Athens founds the Delian League.

336 BC Alexander the Great rules Greece and the islands.

31 BC The Romans annex all Greek territory.

AD 95 St John writes *Revelation* on Patmos

323 Constantine founds the Byzantine Empire; two churches develop, the Orthodox in Constantinople, and the Catholic in Rome.

800–1000 Muslim forces attack the islands.

10th–12th centuries Holy Crusades lead to the break-up of Byzantium.

1204 Venice colonises Crete and the Cyclades; the Genoese take Chios and Lesvos.

1309 The Knights of St John take the Dodecanese islands.

1450–1566 The Ottomans take first Constantinople (renaming it Istanbul), then the Dodecanese islands and, finally, Chios.

1821 Greek War of Independence. Ottomans crush any opposition.

1832 The Cyclades and Sporades are included in the new Greek state.

1912–1913 The Balkans War sees Greece taking the northern and eastern Aegean islands from Turkey. The Dodecanese islands are ceded to Italy.

1939–44 Greece sides with the Allies after being attacked by Italian forces.

1944–49 Civil war in Greece largely bypasses the islands.

1947 The Dodecanese islands are ceded to Greece.

1967–74 Military dictatorship; massive emigration results.

1982 Greece joins the European Common Market (now European Union).

1994 Tensions between Greece and Turkey over territorial rights.

1996 Death of Andreas Papandreou, the socialist prime minister.

2002 Introduction of the euro.

2003 Greece prepares for the 2004 Olympic Games in Athens.

WHERE TO GO

Finding the most suitable Greek island for your style of holiday is important, as each group of islands, as well as each individual island, is unique. Do you want sun-kissed beaches, non-stop nightlife, ancient sites to explore, or traditional Greek family life around you?

Most islands will have a little of each of these elements, but some, such as Ios, have given themselves over almost completely to party tourism. In summer, there is little traditional activity for you to enjoy. Equally, islands such as Lesvos or Chios have few nightclubs. Here you'll find much more evidence of the rural life, with olive groves and livestock farms in the hilly interiors.

In this edition, we have divided the Aegean Islands into five groups. The odyssey starts with the Cyclades islands, the most accessible island chain from Athens, mainland Greece. Travelling counterclockwise, we reach the Dodecanese islands in the southeastern Aegean (excluding Rhodes, which is covered in its own *Pocket Guide*). We then move on to the eastern Aegean islands of Samos, Chios and Lesvos, which sit parallel to the Turkish mainland, and the northern Aegean islands of Samothraki, Limnos and Thassos. We conclude with the Sporades islands of Skiathos, Skopelos, Alonissos and remote Skyros.

Getting Around

Connections among the island chains are poor, with the exception of the ports of Piraeus and Rafina on the Greek mainland, which serve as transportation hubs for those who wish to travel from one chain of islands to another. However,

Architecture on Santorini.

within each chain (particularly the Cyclades, the Dode-canese and the Sporades), ferry connections are regular and journey times are relatively short. Car ferries are the slowest of the transport options, but their stately progress allows you to enjoy the sun and sea air from their promenade and sun decks. Both hydrofoils and large, powerful catamarans will cut ferry journey times in half; however you will sit in an air-conditioned cabin for the duration of your journey.

Once on a particular island, you can easily get around on foot or rent a car for more in-depth exploring. Also, most towns on smaller islands are linked by a good bus system.

Within the Cyclades, Dodecanese and Sporades island groups, there are certain towns that serve as hubs for travel to and from other islands within each group. Below is a list of the hubs and the islands that can be reached by ferry from them within two hours. From Mykonos, you can travel to Delos, Paros, Naxos, Tinos, Andros and Syros. From Skiathos, you can reach Skopelos, Alonissos and Skyros, while from Kos, you can reach Patmos, Kalymnos, Nyssiros and the medieval citadel at Rhodes (covered in the *Pocket Guide to Rhodes*).

The overseas offices of the Greek National Tourist Organ-isation (GNTO) carry current schedules for the major ferry services. The website <www.gtpnet.com> also lists this information. Extra ferries always operate during peak season.

When to Go

The Aegean has a short, wet spring when walking, hiking and mountain biking are extremely enjoyable activities, be-cause the weather is pleasant but not too hot. The air is bright and clear – perfect for photography. However, travel arrangements can be difficult early in the season. The tradi-tional opening time for many hotels is the Orthodox Easter, although some do not open until the end of April. The ferries operate a winter – which means 'curtailed' – service until the first week in May.

Summers on the islands are long and hot, but the heat is tempered (or disguised) by the sometimes blustery Meltemi winds, which blow from the heart of central Asia, south through the Aegean. The summer season is also marked by an influx of backpackers and package holiday-makers from all across Europe. The islands are busy, but all facilities such as hotels and restaurants are open, and the number of extra ferries and small boats (known as caiques) provide more opportunity to travel between the islands.

Day-tripping in style on a local caique in Mykonos.

Autumn tends to be warm, with a less frantic pace than in summer – perfect for watching such activities as the harvesting of the olives. By the middle of October, the season is over and many hotels and restaurants will close for the winter. Most of the staff you'll see in bars and hotels during the summer return to their homes on mainland Greece until spring the following year.

THE CYCLADES

Lying closest to Athens and the Attic peninsula, the Cyclades is the island chain that most people think of as archetypally Greek. Its islands have small fishing harbours replete with azure water, whitewashed houses with brightly coloured trims, small domed chapels, and donkeys in the fields.

Originally named many centuries ago because its islands formed a circle or *cyclos* around the island of Delos – one of the most important sites in the ancient world – the Cyclades was first composed of a dozen islands. Twenty islands have since been added, making the Cyclades the largest of the Greek island groups.

You will definitely find yourself sharing the main islands with many other visitors, although this has not yet spoiled their charms. For those who look for solitude, there are still quiet islands to be explored, off the beaten track.

Mykonos

A tiny, treeless rocky island regularly swept by summer winds has become one of the most popular holiday destinations in the Mediterranean. Why? **Mykonos** is a state of mind as well as a place. It's hedonistic and funky, and tolerant of alternative lifestyles. A mecca for gay travellers and nude sunbathers, Mykonos is also a trendy spot for the

---

Petros the Mascot

One year, four pelicans on their annual migration between the Black Sea and Egypt were blown off-course in a storm and forced to land on Mykonos. Three of them subsequently died, but the fourth, Petros, survived and was adopted by a fisherman, Theodoros.

In 1985 the original Petros was involved in a fatal car accident. However, the following year, another pelican – donated to the island by a German businessman – appeared on Mykonos. He was named Petros in honour of his unfortunate predecessor. Today, that Petros lives on the quayside, patrolling among the boats for his next fishy meal, his beautiful pink feathers scattering the harbour.

fabulous and well-connected, who come to shop in its designer boutiques (open almost around the clock) and go clubbing until sunrise.

Amazingly, the island retains its Greek character. The capital, **Mykonos Town**, is one of the most beautiful in the Aegean. The island happily caters to families in addition to single travellers, and backpackers as well as the wealthy. It offers a stepping stone to the sacred island of Delos, with all its archaeological treasures, yet has a variety of beaches for those who want to do little but soak in the sun.

Petros II, the pelican mascot of Mykonos Town.

Mykonos Town is the only large settlement on the island. It's built on undulating land that radiates out from a fishing harbour where a small fleet still moors and sells its catch. You will probably encounter the island mascot **Petros**, a pelican waddling among the boats, hoping to find a fishy titbit. Beside the port sits the quaint, round-domed **Paraportiani Church**, a favourite backdrop for fashion photographers.

Behind the port is a maze of narrow alleys and whitewashed houses with overhanging balconies resplendent with potted plants and masses of bougainvillea. Art galleries, jewellers and fashionable eateries can be found on every corner; but early in the morning you'll have the streets to yourself to enjoy every detail of the pretty Cycladic architecture. Brightly painted doors hide cool courtyards, and white paint outlines the stone pavements of the alleyways. A small bay

Waterside drinks in the Alefkandra Quarter (Little Venice), Mykonos.

bounding the north side of town has Venetian balconies overhanging the water. Known as the **Alefkandra Quarter** or 'Little Venice', it is the place to come for a sunset cocktail or dinner by the water's edge. From here, you'll get a full view of the distinctive five **windmills** that sit in a row overlooking the town.

Walking from the fishing harbour north towards the commercial port will take you past the small **Folklore Museum**, with exhibits of traditional Greek household items. Nearby, next to the southern bus station, is the **archaeological museum**. Among its many exhibits, there are funerary statues and other items from the island of Rhenia, the burial ground for the inhabitants of Delos.

The interior of Mykonos is barren and dusty. The only buildings that break the monotony are the more than 300 small white chapels that dot the hillsides. Centre of worship on the island is the red-roofed **Tourliani Monastery** with its

16th-century bell towers. It is situated at the heart of the inland village of Ano Mera, whose small square makes a peaceful place for a leisurely lunch.

The beaches of Mykonos rival those of St Tropez in their reputation for bohemian activities; however, there are enough stretches of sand and little coves that you can find somewhere that suits your own tastes. **Paradise Beach**, a clothing-optional beach, is probably the most famous, with non-stop music that lasts well into the early hours of the morning. **Super-Paradise**, in the next bay, is a gay, clothing-optional beach. Families head out to **Platis Gialos** or **Psarou**, but they can be crowded. Further east, **Elia** and **Agia Anna** offer the promise of a little more space.

Delos

It is difficult to over-estimate the importance of the sacred island of **Delos** during ancient times. According to Greek myth, it was the birthplace of Apollo, God of Light. It was believed to be free floating until Apollo's birth, after which huge columns rose up from the sea bed to anchor the island. Perhaps because of its geographical location at the centre of the islands in the surrounding Cyclades group, it also inspired the name for the island chain. (Cyclades, you may remember, comes from *cyclos*, or circle.) Delos was not only an important religious centre, but also a major meeting point for trade between East and West during the Hellenistic and Roman eras. It was designated the home of the treasury of the Delian League in 480 BC, an act which encouraged its growth as a centre for banking and commerce. As a result, Delos is now one of the most important archaeological sites in the world. Its remains reflect its dual roles in ancient Greek life, a holy place and a centre of trade.

Today, Delos has no modern settlement or tourist infra-structure. Visitors must travel here by boat, as an excursion from a surrounding island, alighting at a small jetty beside the ancient port, now silted up. From here, the vista of the whole town can be seen, with a fine residential quarter to the right, and the remains of a series of magnificent temples to the left. The temples were the last stop on a long pilgrimage for ancient Greek believers. Here, you could make offerings to the god Apollo at his birthplace, or consult the powerful oracle in residence.

From the ferry jetty, turn left and walk down the **Sacred Way**. In the distance, you will see a fine palm tree, a symbol of Apollo's birthplace. Surrounding it are the remains of the **Sacred Lake**, drained in the 1920s to prevent mosquitoes from breeding in the stagnant water. Walking through the site towards the palm tree will take you past the **Sanctuary of Apollo**, comprising a series of once-fine, colonnaded stoas and temples, including one to Apollo's sister, Artemis.

A number of lion statues, the **Terrace of the Lions**, form a guard of honour on the approach to the sacred lake. They are perhaps the most photographed symbol of Delos, and are

---

The Birthplace of Apollo

The little island of Delos in the heart of the Cyclades is home to an ancient site of outstanding importance. According to legend it was here that the Leto gave birth to Apollo, son of Zeus. For almost 1,000 years, the sanctuary remained the political and religious centre of the Aegean, attracting pilgrims from far and wide and holding, every four years, one of the largest festivals in Ancient Greece. The Romans, however, turned the island into a grand trade fair and made it into a free port; it also became Greece's slave market, where up to 10,000 slaves were reputed to be sold in one day. By the Christian era, the influence of Delos was waning, and until the arrival of French archeologists in 1870 the island was forgotten. Nowadays, Delos is an archeologist's paradise.

believed to date from the seventh century BC. Their numbers have dwindled over the centuries from 16 to only five. Today, an attempt is being made to recreate the statues in their prime, with modern materials. At present, only one is in its natural aged state.

On higher ground behind the lake is the **Museum of Delos**. Although it has the dour look of a barracks building, it houses many of the finest statuary and artefacts found at the site, and

Sixteen marble lions once stood guard over the Sacred Lake.

they bring to life the bare bones of the temple buildings and houses. Fine pottery and exquisite jewellery show that daily life was enhanced by quality possessions, which were taken for granted by the population.

To the left of the temple area is perhaps one of the most exciting parts of Delos, the **Theatre Quarter**, although the theatre itself (third century BC) is not the highlight of the site. It is the labyrinth of family houses in its shadow that brings the city to life. Streets that have felt the footfalls of ancient Greeks and Romans still lead to the front doors of their homes and shops. Some are simply meagre square boxes, but behind a number of strong stone walls, magnificent homes are revealed. Interior courtyards were beautified by some of the most ornate mosaic floors and wall frescoes in the ancient world.

Search out the **House of Dionysos** and the **House of the Trident**, with their simple floor patterns, and the **House of**

TΡAΣ
ΟΡΑΤRE

At home with Cleopatra and her husband's headless statues.

Dolphins and the **House of Masks** for more elaborate examples, including Dionysos riding a panther, on the floor of the House of Masks.

The **House of Cleopatra** is also worthy of note, named after the lady of the house who left behind headless statues of herself and her husband, Dioskourides. The statues *in situ* are reproductions – the originals sit in the Delos Museum.

Behind the Theatre Quarter is an area with a number of shrines dedicated to foreign gods, an indication of the numerous cultures that influenced Delos. Syrian and Egyptian gods were worshipped here.

Above the town, the slopes of Mount Kynthos rise to a height of 112 m (367 ft), offering a view across the whole site. The climb – along a narrow and sometimes steep path – will lead to scant remains of third-century BC temples, although the site was occupied as early as the Stone Age.

Lying a few hundred metres to the west, the island of **Rhenia** was both a birthplace for Delians and their burial ground. Delos was a sacred island and its soil had to be kept pure; therefore, birth and death were prohibited human activities. Even today this ancient code is still being kept by modern archaeologists. Funerary artefacts found here are displayed in Mykonos.

Andros

The nearest Cyclades island to the Greek mainland, **Andros** is a short ferry ride from the port of Rafina, and is therefore popular with Athenians. Wealthy shipping families own large houses along the coast and in the hills, which are more verdant than those of other islands in the group, and its red soil contrasts with the dull earth of Mykonos or Paros.

The major port of **Gavrion** on the west coast serves the whole island, but the main town is **Chora** (which simply means 'town', and is often used on islands with only one main settlement). Off the tourist route, on the east coast of the island, it is also known as **Andros Town**. Much of Chora has remained unchanged for decades, as Athenian week-enders have refurbished the charming old townhouses, and it has a very genteel air.

The cultural heart of Andros owes much to the generosity of the Goulandris shipping family. They funded the **Modern Art Museum**, to the north of the square, which features the work of a selection of European modernist painters. They were also instrumental in the creation of the **archaeological museum** that houses the Hermes of Andros, a second-century copy of a statue originally sculpted by Praxiteles.

The main resort is **Batsi** on the west coast, just south of Gavrion. The small centre still retains vestiges of its heritage as a fishing village, but modern hotels and apartments have been built on the outskirts. The **Monastery of Zoodohos Pighi** (Life-giving Spring) lies in the hills above Batsi and guards the most sacred of several freshwater springs found on the island.

Tinos

The island of **Tinos** is a surprise because it is a centre of Roman Catholic worship in an Orthodox land. This is in part because it remained under Catholic Venetian rule far longer than other islands in the Aegean – from 1207 to 1714 – but also because it was the scene of a blessed miracle, ensuring its fame throughout the Catholic community in Greece. In 1823, a nun from the Convent of Kechrovouni had a dream in which the Virgin Mary told her that a sacred icon could be found in land nearby. The nun went out and found the portrait just as her dream had foretold. Since that time, the icon has been held responsible for many feats of healing, giving Tinos the epithet 'Lourdes of Greece'. The island is a delight, because it has few foreign visitors and retains its strong Greek character.

The capital of the island, **Tinos Town**, houses the icon in the **Panagia Evangelistria**, a church that sits at the top of a gentle slope rising up from the port 1 km (0.6 miles) away. The icon has a powerful influence over pilgrims, who crawl up the church steps on their hands and knees to pray for divine intervention. Two major festivals, Annunciation Day on 25 March and Assumption Day on 15 August, see thousands of believers crawling up the hill from the port to worship the icon. Don't travel to the island at either of these times without a reservation.

Pilgrims flock to Tinos to worship its icon.

Travel into the countryside and you'll soon see how hilly Tinos is. Hundreds of terraces cover the slopes, giving them a textured look. Today, many lie overgrown and unused, but in Venetian times, they brimmed with crops and grew fodder for livestock. They are made accessible by thousands of narrow donkey tracks, which are used by hikers and ramblers.

Scattered throughout the land are hundreds of **dove-cotes**, which were introduced across the Aegean by the Venetians, who enjoyed pigeon as a part of their diet. On other islands, the towers have been allowed to decay, but on Tinos they stand proud, many with birds still in residence. Some of the most accessible can be found near the village of **Tarabados**, 8 km (13 miles) north of Tinos Town.

The ground rises dramatically behind Tinos Town to a rocky peak known as **Exobourgo**. Here, you can see the remains of a vast Venetian fortress destroyed by invading Ottoman forces.

Nest with a view – custom-made Venetian dovecotes on Tinos.

Wander, at your own risk, among the walls, crumbling turrets, and caves, and look out towards the surrounding islands of Mykonos and Andros. In the shadow of the peak is a network of villages, unspoiled both by the influence of tourists and the excesses of modern life. One of the prettiest, **Dyo Chorio**, has fresh spring water fountains which are still used by hill farmers to collect water for their homes. Village households still wash their laundry in these waters.

The central section of Tinos has little of interest, but make your way over the hills to the pretty village of **Pyrgos**, famed for its school of marble carving. The village, nestled into a narrow valley, is one of the prettiest in the Aegean. A number of craftsmen have studios fronting onto the narrow streets. From Pyrgos, head down to the fishing port of **Panormos**, 3 km (2 miles) away, where you can enjoy delicious fresh fish at one of the many tavernas.

Sifnos

In ancient times, **Sifnos** was renowned for its gold and silver deposits. The island's treasury, stored at Delphi (the most important sanctuary in ancient Greece) was said to be the richest of the many deposited there. In more recent times, wealth has passed Sifnos by, but it still produces some jewellery and has a reputation for particularly fine pottery, which can be seen outside the workshops drying in the sun. The island also has an amazing 365 churches and monasteries nestled among its abundant olive groves.

The main port, **Kamares**, lies 5 km (3 miles) from the capital **Apollonia**, and its sister town **Artemon** (both named for the brother and sister god and goddess of ancient Greek mythology). The oldest continually occupied settlement on the island is **Kastro**, where most of the buildings date from the 14th century and were laid out in a circular pattern atop a rocky outcrop 100 m (300 ft) above the east coast. The town is a fascinating mix of crumbling grandeur and renovated splendour. An **archaeological museum** is housed in a building of Venetian origin and contains finds from the Mycenaean and Archaic periods. The main beaches of Sifnos lie on the south coast. **Platis Gialos** is popular with a range of bars and tavernas, but **Vathi** is perhaps the most visually stunning, with the now deconsecrated

Built in 1653 Hrysopighi Monastery has an icon with allegedly miraculous powers. It once destroyed the stone bridge leading to the islet, saving the monastery from pirate attack, and later saved Sifnos from plague.

17th-century **Hrysopighi Monastery** set on a small offshore island, which is reached by a bridge.

Paros and Antiparos

Paros, a major ferry junction, is an island with something for almost everyone. Across a narrow channel sits Antiparos (meaning 'opposite Paros'), with a main settlement that takes you back to the Greek Islands of 20 years ago. The capital of Paros, **Parikia**, serves the port, and although it is very busy during peak season, it still retains the feel of a Greek town. Away from the port, a maze of narrow streets disguise the remains

Shopping in the narrow winding streets of Parikia, Paros.

of a kastro, or castle, dating from the 13th century, which recycled marble from Greek and Roman temples on the island.

To the left of the port, beside the new medical centre, is the **Panagia Ekatontapiliani**, known as the **Church of 100 Doors**. The present buildings are based around a 4th-century structure that is said to have been commissioned by St Helen, mother of Constantine the Great (founder of Constantinople and the leader who converted the Roman Empire to Christianity), and the 6th-century chapel uses columns from an earlier Roman temple.

Nearby, the **archaeological museum** has a section of the Parian Chronicles, a history of ancient Greece enscribed on marble slabs, along with other examples of Paros marble, which was coveted throughout the ancient world for its fine translucence.

Leave Parikia behind and Paros has a number of villages to explore. In the north, **Naoussa** has one of the prettiest fishing harbours in the Mediterranean. Although popular with visitors, it has not lost its traditional industry. Boats in daily use lie within feet of the fashionable bars and restaurants. It's no surprise that the harbour has some of the best seafood restaurants in the Aegean, including several traditional Greek ouzeries. To the west of Naoussa is **Kolymbithres**, a growing resort whose beaches are surrounded by strange rock features that are folded by immense natural forces and eroded by the wind. The resort has a large park featuring water slides and a children's play area.

> The Church of 100 Doors has, in fact, only 99 known doors. Local folklore states that when the 100th door is found it will signal a resurgence of the Byzantine Orthodox Empire and the return of its first city, Constantinople (now Istanbul), to Greek hands.

Along the eastern coastline are several fine beaches with perfect windsurfing conditions in their wide, shallow bays. The World Windsurfing Championships have been held here in August for the last several years. **Golden Beach** is perfect for soaking up the sun and watching the sport. Further along the east coast is the pretty port of **Piso Livadi**.

The interior of the island has a number of interesting attractions. **Lefkes** village occupies high ground in the interior, and its narrow streets are perfect places to explore. Look out for the remains of a marble-covered Byzantine road (fourth to 14th-century) that once connected Lefkes with the nearby village of **Karampoli** down in the valley.

Near the village of **Marathi** you will find the ancient marble quarries that sent stone to all parts of the Greek and Roman empires. The stone was mined rather than cut from the surface, and the tunnels can be explored with a flashlight. The building remains you'll see once housed French workmen who came here in 1844 to cut marble for Napoleon's tomb in the Hôtel des Invalides in Paris. If you visit Paros in July or August, take a trip to **Petaloudes** (the Valley of the Butterflies) south of Parikia, a breeding ground for giant tiger moths, which cling to the leaves of trees in vast numbers.

A fisherman checks his nets in Naoussa harbour, Paros.

Until 5,000 years ago **Antiparos** was attached to Paros, but seismic activity and climatic change have produced a narrow sea channel with several tiny islands between the two. Antiparos can be reached by a 20-minute ferry ride from Parikia, or a five-minute car ferry trip from the small port of **Pounda** on Paros's western coast. The town of Antiparos seems to move at a slower pace than Parikia; in fact, the town can be almost somnolent out of season. At its heart is a **Venetian kastro** that still retains original dwelling houses along its interior walls.

The main attractions on the island are the **caves** under the mountain of Agios Ilias in the south. The interior is cavernous,

A quiet spot for relaxation on Antiparos.

but the caves have suffered from centuries of vandalism. The number of steps built down into the interior means that they are unsuitable for the infirm or those with heart problems.

Naxos

The largest island in the Cyclades, **Naxos** is a place of contrasts. It has barren hills, mountain ranges and green fertile valleys that produce grapes and olives in abundance. The island has a long history; its marble deposits were coveted around the ancient world. In fact, the Lions of Delos were made from Naxos marble. The wonderful beaches along the western coast were, until recently, a secret, but they have now been discovered. Tourism has grown over the last 10 years.

The capital of Naxos, **Hora**, sits on the western coastline and is served by a rather breezy but extremely busy port. There is a wide promenade along the seafront with cafés and restaurants, but the heart of the magnificent old town lies just above this, overlooking the harbour, and comprises a labyrinth of alleyways and narrow streets around a Venetian citadel, which caps the highest point. Small Byzantine churches sit on street corners, side by side with family homes. The church of **Panagia Theoskepastos** houses a fine 14th-century icon, and the **Catholic Cathedral** has a 10th-century Madonna and Child. Next door to the cathedral is the **archaeological museum** with finds from every era of Naxos's long history.

On a rocky promontory beside the town is the site of the **Temple of Apollo**, dating from the sixth century BC. It was planned as the largest temple in the Aegean, but was never completed. Only the giant portal, 5.5 m (18 ft) tall, was in place when work stopped, but it gives an indication of how immense the whole task would have been.

The interior of Naxos offers a range of environments not found on other islands of the Aegean. Fertile valleys with precious water supplies offer a cool and fragrant break from the heat of the towns and beaches. The valley between the towns of **Chalki** and **Filoti** (known as the **Tragea Valley**) is perhaps the most beautiful, and easily reached by bus from Hora. Ancient olive groves play host to donkeys and herds of goats, and low-growing vines cover the ground under tall Cypress trees – the archetypal Greek landscape. The heart of Chalki hides a Venetian tower and the whole valley has a number of small Byzantine chapels.

A busy causeway, connecting Hora, the capital of Naxos.

Filoti sits in the shadow of **Mount Zas**, a treeless brown rock rising from the green valley below. Although you can't climb to the summit, there are beautiful walks or cycle paths on its lower slopes, with caves to explore and cooling streams to enjoy.

Travelling north out of the Tragea Valley past villages seemingly clinging to the valley sides, **Keramoti**, **Koronos** and **Korinada** are all

The marble door frame to the Temple of Apollo, Naxos.

fascinating places to explore. All give glimpses of traditional family life. A small resort on the northern coast, Apollon, holds a fascinating artefact from the past. A giant block of marble, formed into a *kouros* (male statue) more than 2,600 years ago lies prostrate on the ground. The marble cracked before the figure was finished and it was abandoned where it lay.

The best sandy beaches of Naxos lie on the sheltered west coast to the south of Chora. **Agia Anna**, and the long sandy spit of **Agios Prokopios** are two of the most popular.

Amorgos

The narrow 18-km (11-miles) long island of **Amorgos** lies to the southwest of Naxos and attracts those in search of peace and tranquillity. It is dominated by a mountain range rising to 822 m (2,696 ft).

The harbour town of **Katapola** occupies a small coastal plain. Trees overhang the quayside and orchards surround the town. At **Minoa**, just above Katapola, the scant ruins of a gymnasium, stadium and temple to Apollo are all that remain of a once important ancient city.

Inland, the elevated **Amorgos Town**, also known as **Hora**, is a charming cluster of whitewashed houses and numerous churches around a 13th-century Venetian castle and a row of windmills. To the northeast, perched on the side of a 180-m (590-ft) high cliff overlooking the Aegean, is the spectacular 11th-century **Monastery of Panagia Hozoviotissa**, one of the most beautiful in Greece. It is home to a revered icon of the Virgin from Palestine.

The most accessible beaches on the island are along the northwest coast at Katapola and **Ormos Aighiali**.

Santorini

The island of **Santorini** (Thira) is one of the must-see places of the world, for no other reason than because it frames the earth's largest **volcanic caldera**. Santorini looked exactly like many of the other islands in the Cyclades until around 1500 BC, when a massive eruption of its volcano carried the whole interior of the island high into the atmosphere, changing the climate of the earth for years afterwards. In place of land came water, surging in to fill the 11-km (7-mile) long void and causing massive tidal waves around the Mediterranean Sea.

What remains today is the outer rim of the original circular island. Sheer cliffs up to 300 m (984 ft) high bound the caldera, and a number of whitewashed settlements nestle along their crests, looking from a distance like icing melting down the sides of a cake. Another section of the original island sits to the west. **Thirasia** now has separate settlements that can be visited by ferry from Santorini.

In the centre of the caldera are two low-lying areas of land that appeared after the 1500 BC eruption: **Nea Kameni** and **Palea Kameni**. Because the volcano is still active – although dormant at present – these areas continue to grow, and experience earthquakes. The last major one occurred in 1956 and inflicted a great deal of damage to the towns on the main island.

The town of Fira, Santorini, perched on the edge of the caldera.

The main town of the island is **Fira**, set atop the high cliffs in the centre of the long interior curve. Its buildings tumble down towards the water with stunning views. A narrow cobbled trail of 587 steps leads from the town to the small port below, now the domain of a fleet of donkeys that wait to carry cruise ship passengers into town. For those who would prefer a quicker method, there is a cable car that wings you from sea level to the cliffs in a couple of minutes. Most commercial ferries arrive at the new port of **Athinios** further along the coast.

Fira is a shopper's paradise, a series of narrow alleys where you can wander free from the fear of traffic, although keep your eyes and ears open for donkeys. You can buy anything from a reproduction icon to a genuine Fabergé egg, plus jewellery of the finest quality and designer clothing by the most desirable names. Find a spot for a drink at sunset (which has to be one of the most spectacular on earth).

Among the boutiques and bars are two places of cultural interest. The **archaeological museum** on a square next to the cable car station (a new building is under construction near the main bus station, which will eventually house the collection) features pottery and other artefacts found on the island. The **Megaron Gyzi Museum**, located to the north of the cable car station, is housed in a beautiful 17th-century fortified house. Most notable of its varied collections is a display of photographs showing island scenes from before the devastating 1956 earthquake.

Fira is beautiful, but it can become oppressive when visitors crowd the narrow streets. A little way north is another smaller town where the pace is less frantic. **Ia** (pronounced Oya), set on the northern cliffs, became home to a number of artists early on, and it maintains a more bohemian atmosphere than Fira. There are many homes built into the steep hillsides; some have been converted into art galleries and shops selling collectibles. The architecture is typical of the Cyclades, and the buildings' multicoloured façades make it one of the world's most photographed villages.

Aside from the stunning views, Santorini has much more to show its visitors. In the centre of the island is the village of **Pirgos**, with the remains of a Venetian fortress at its heart. On a rocky bluff beyond the village you will find the 17th-century **Monastery of Profitis Ilias**. As the road climbs towards the entrance, you'll pass fields full of Santorini's renowned tomatoes growing on the steep slopes. The monastery is only open

> Having arrived on Santorini, visitors are often surprised to see, beyond the steep caldera to the east, coastal plains that are covered in a blanket of vines. In fact, more than 100,000 bottles of wine are produced on the island every year and exported worldwide.

when the priests inside take liturgies (mornings and early evenings), but it is well worth taking the time to visit. Pride of place goes to a 15th-century icon of the prophet Elijah.

The monastery also has a museum, which conveys the flavour of monastic life along with icons and manuscripts. Unfortunately, the hilltop is also shared by the Greek military, and it bristles with satellite and digital technology, prohibiting photography of the beautiful panorama.

On the northern slopes of this rocky outcrop is the site of the ancient capital of the island, also called **Thira**, which dates from the third century BC (when the Aegean was under Ptolemaic rule). The site sprawls over a wide area, but some remains are in poor condition, a situation that causes the site to close intermittently because of the danger of falling masonry. Check with the tourist board in Fira before setting out.

In the south of the island is one of the most important ancient sites in the Mediterranean. Near the modern village

---

A Cluster of Tiny Islands

In addition to the islands mentioned in this chapter, the Cyclades also includes numerous tiny islands that remain off the main tourist track.

Milos, where the *Venus de Milo* (now a prize exhibit at the Louvre, Paris) was discovered, reached its peak during the Bronze Age, when obsidian found on the island was used for the manufacture of primitive utensils, sparking off trade in the region. Nowadays, the strange rock formations on Milos continue to fascinate geologists.

Syros, the capital of the Cyclades, is the only Aegean island on which modern towns have been established and with a proper sense of urbanisation.

The tiny, so-called 'Back Islands' of **Donoussa**, **Iraklia** and **Shinoussa**, south-east of Naxos, have populations of only 100 to 200 each. **Keros** is totally uninhabited and boats do not even travel there.

of **Akrotiri**, a complete city dating from before 2000 BC was discovered. It was buried under several feet of ash during the eruption of c.1500 BC, but unlike the tragic city of Pompeii in Italy, no human remains have been found. This has led scientists to believe that the population escaped before the disaster took place.

Since 1967, the site has been painstakingly excavated to give a picture of daily life before the great eruption. A society of complexity and sophistication has been unveiled, one that had urban planning, heating, sanitation and a standard script. However, much of

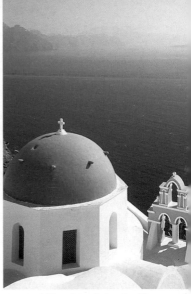

A blue-domed church with extraordinary views.

the beautiful artwork found here is now in the archaeological museum in Athens. The site is still an active dig and new discoveries are being made all the time. The remains, which include streets with houses and pretty communal squares, have been placed under a protective, corrugated roof and the site becomes hot and crowded, so try to visit as early in the day as possible.

The beaches of Santorini are made of fine black or red volcanic sand, which heats to a ferocious temperature in the summer sun. **Kamari** and **Perissa** are growing resorts with a range of hotels, bars, and restaurants. Both make pleasant retreats after a day of sightseeing in Fira or Akrotiri.

Some of the best views of Santorini are from the water. Try taking a trip around the caldera, with stops at the new volcanic islands of Nea and Palea Kameni. Allow time in Thirasia to explore Santorini's smaller sibling islands.

Ios

Ios is the undisputed party island of the Aegean, and its bars and clubs boom out the latest dance tunes 24 hours a day. Traditionally a poor island, the native population has happily embraced the new seasonal lifestyle that has brought them prosperity, and the old ways of life have almost completely disappeared. Arriving by boat, you'll have splendid views of the magnificent unspoiled, treeless landscape, which bears scant evidence of the hand of man. Only the southeastern corner has any real development, and the road system comprises less than 10 km (16 miles) from the pretty, narrow streets of **Chora**, the island's only town, to the beach at **Milopotamos** in the neighbouring bay.

Milopotamos is one of the best and busiest beaches in the Aegean. This leaves a whole island to explore on foot, or by 4-wheel-drive vehicle. Residents of Ios will tell you that an ancient tomb in the north of the island is that of Homer, author of *The Odyssey* and *The Iliad* (his mother was born on Ios). Unfortunately, no positive proof has ever corroborated the claim.

THE DODECANESE

The Dodecanese islands take their name from the Greek phrase *dodeka nisi*, meaning 12 islands, although the group incorporates far more than one dozen in its number. Over the years, their nationality has changed several times: until 1912 they were part of the Ottoman Empire, from 1912 to 1947 they were ruled by Italy and in 1947 they were passed into Greek hands. The major islands exhibit faded remains of a

Muslim influence, though this was just one of several cultures to leave its mark on the region.

Kos

Now the second most-populated island in the Dodecanese, **Kos** has seen human settlement since ancient times. With safe harbours and wide fertile plains, it could both protect and feed its people. Today it is very popular with package holiday-makers, particularly high-spirited young Europeans. Try to visit early or late in the season to avoid the crowds and their worst excesses.

Kos Town on the western coast is the main settlement and a fascinating place to explore. Settled for many centuries, it suffered an earthquake in 1933 that damaged much of the modern town centre, but allowed Italian archaeologists to excavate a large section of the Roman city which lay directly

A hydrofoil approaches Ios harbour.

underneath. Today it is possible to walk through the old *agora* (marketplace) and stroll along Roman roads.

Later, after the fall of Jerusalem, the town became a stronghold of the Knights of St John. In the 15th century, they built the **Castle of the Knights of St John** at the water's edge. It still forms an impressive backdrop for photographs of Mandraki Harbour, and is filled with items of historical 'litter', including carved marble plaques, statuary and cannons.

Ottoman forces ousted the knights in 1522, and evidence of their stay can be found just inland from the castle. The minaret of the **Loggia Mosque**, built in the 18th century and the largest on Kos, now stands silent and closed, but it is matched by a number of smaller examples throughout town, some still in use by the small Muslim population.

Beside the mosque – in fact, almost overshadowing it – is a large plane tree. Its branches extend so far that it has had to be supported for many years by a framework of scaffolding. The local people will tell you that this is the **Hippocrates Tree**, under which the father of medicine, a native of the island, lectured to his students more than 2,500 years ago. Sadly, although the tree has been proved to be among the oldest in Europe, most experts believe that it is only 2,000 years old and therefore not of Hippocrates' era. In the main square of the town (walk inland from the mosque on the south side of the *agora*) is the **archaeological museum**, which features finds from ancient Kos, including mosaics and domestic utensils. On the outskirts of town, situated on E Grigorou Street, is a small **Roman Odeon** or theatre, used in summer for performances. Nearby is **Casa Romana**, a Roman villa recreated in every detail. It really brings to life the daily routines of a wealthy Roman family.

If you don't want to walk around town, a small motorised train runs past all the major sites. The train operates several times a day during the summer months.

Situated four kilometres (2½ miles) outside Kos Town are the remains of a medical school founded during the fourth century BC, shortly after the death of Hippocrates. The **Asclepium** was a major centre of healing. Many of the largest remains date from the Roman, rather than the Classical Greek era, and the site was damaged by the Knights of St. John when they removed marble from it to build their castle. The main Doric temple rested on the upper level of the three terraces that make up the site. There are fine views across to Turkey.

The mighty ramparts of the Castle of the Knights of St John, Kos.

Resorts outside Kos Town include **Kardamena** on the south coast, a young, energetic centre; **Tigaki** on the north coast, a quiet resort more suited to couples and families; and **Kamari**, which lies the furthest from Kos Town. All offer a selection of hotels, bars and restaurants.

The flat landscape, especially in the east, is ideal for cycling, where you can get away and explore such inland villages as **Pyli** (and the older **Paleo Pyli** high in the hills), **Asfendiou** and **Kefalos**, with the last working windmill on the island. Here you can still find a quiet spot to enjoy authentic Greek island life.

Nissyros

Legend has that while Poseidon, the Greek God of the Sea, was pursuing the Titan Polyvotis, the former tore a rock from nearby Kos and crushed his adversary beneath it. The rock became **Nissyros**. The groaning of the Titan is said still to be audible beneath the surface of the caldera in Nissyros's most impressive feature, the **volcano** that forms the heart of the island. Infrequent buses make the trip from Mandhraki harbour to the crater 13 km (8 miles) to the southeast. With stout shoes you can visit the caldera floor, braving the rotten-egg stench caused by sulphur.

Hippocrate's Tree and the minaret of the Loggia Mosque, Kos.

Yellow crystals form around hissing steam vents while mud boils out of sight – supposedly the voice of Polyvotis.

The main town of **Mandhraki** features tall white houses houses with colourful wooden balconies arranged around a central communal orchard. Overhead, the Knights' castle shelters the **Monastery of Panagia Spiliani**, while to the south lies the Doric citadel of **Paleokastro**. Walking trails allow you to explore the green interior of the island.

Patmos

This small, barren island in the northern Dodecanese may have remained the deserted outpost it once was, had it not been for a decision in the first century AD to use it as a penal colony for political and religious dissidents. It was here in AD 95 that one resident received divine inspiration in the form of an apocalyptic vision while he sat in his small cave high above the harbour. The words that John the Theologian (Evangelist in Greek) recorded became *Revelation* (Apocalypse in Greek), the last book of the New Testament.

In 1088, the Byzantine Emperor ceded land on the island to a monk, Christodoulos, who founded a monastery here in honour of the saint. It soon became a place of contemplation, learning and pilgrimage – a status that it still holds for thousands of believers to the present day.

Since there is no airport on the island, all visitors must arrive at the port, **Skala**, where most of the hotels are located and all commercial activity is carried out. Despite the num-

> The 11th-century Monastery of St John the Theologian on Patmos was built as a fortress to protect its treasures from pirates. It even has slits for pouring oil over its attackers. The massive buttressed walls were restored after an earthquake in 1956.

ber of visitors passing through, Skala is still a Greek village at heart, with a number of traditional tavernas to be found in the streets around the small main square. A new yacht basin to the east provides a safe harbour for independent travellers.

Everyone who arrives at the port can look up and see their first view of the **Monastery of St John the Theologian**, surrounded by the town of **Chora** atop a nearby hill. The monastery was built at a tumultuous time in Christian history and its design was based on that of a castle, to act as a protection of the faith and its treasures, as well as for worship. It stands high above myriad whitewashed walls.

Monks once ruled Patmos; their presence induces a sense of calm.

In times past pilgrims travelled from the port to the monastery on foot or by donkey via a narrow cobbled track. The path still exists, and in the cool of the early morning, it makes for a pleasant uphill walk. Alternatively, you can take one of the regular buses or a taxi for the 10-minute ride.

Halfway up the hill is the **Convent of the Apocalypse**, at the site of the cave where St John received divine revelation. Now tended by nuns, the convent is regarded as holy ground (follow the same rules of dress expected at other holy places). The small **Cave of St Anne** has a silver band where it is said that John laid his head each night, and a simple rock ledge is said to have been his desk. Two chapels now grace the grounds. On reaching Hora, you will need to walk through the pedestrian-only town to reach the monastery. The streets have an almost eerie emptiness, although in summer small kittens scamper away as you approach, disappearing into cracks in the thick, high walls. Eventually the signposts lead to the strong stone archway that signals the entrance to the Monastery of St John.

Immediately on entering the cobbled main courtyard, you will see a small church on the left, built on the site of an ancient temple of Artemis. Inside you will find the marble sarcophagus of the monastery's founder Christodoulos and icons that date from as early as 1190. Behind the chapel is the 11th-century refectory where it is possible to gain an insight into the daily lives of the generations of monks who made this monastery their home. The utilitarian communal tables and simple decorations offered no distractions from their serious vocation.

Take the staircase in the eastern corner of the courtyard to find the treasury, which exhibits only a fraction of the wealth accumulated by the monastery. Beautifully displayed are a range of icons dating from the 12th century, silver altar pieces and bejewelled vestments. The monastery received bequests from nobility throughout the Orthodox world, and was not averse to making money from commerce, particularly shipping. In this way, it amassed vast fortunes still kept under lock and key.

The library was once one of the most important in the Byzantine world. Large numbers of volumes were evacuated from here before the fall of Constantinople, comprising the

---

Patmos and the End of the World

It is almost as difficult to reach Patmos nowadays as it was in Roman times when the authorities made the island into a penal colony for political prisoners. In AD 95 John the Theologian (as Evangelist is known in Greek), who had been preaching Christianity in Asia Minor (now Turkey), was condemned for crimes against the Emperor and deported here.

The holy man is said to have heard a thunderous voice, like a trumpet, announcing the end of the world and the eventual triumph of Christianity. He recorded what he heard in a grotto on Patmos, and what he recorded became the end to the New Testament – the book known as *Revelation*, or *The Apocalypse*.

best in early Christian decorated manuscripts and books of the Bible. However, the library is only open to scholars and requires prior written permission for research.

Despite the importance of the monastery, a great deal of ordinary life can be seen around Patmos. Small holdings abound, and traditional houses sit low on the treeless hillsides. The beaches on the northern coastline beyond the village of **Kambos** are said to be the best on the island, although some are difficult to reach. Most accessible is **Lampis Bay**, with a couple of good tavernas. South of Skala is the small resort of **Grikos Bay**.

Kalymnos

For centuries, the natives of **Kalymnos** were renowned for their diving prowess. They developed it in order to harvest the sponges that grew abundantly in the seas all around the island. However, the early 20th century saw several catastrophic changes that ruined the commercial sponge industry on Kalymnos. Many families emigrated to the United States and Australia to make new lives, and the natural population dropped dramatically. Although the traditional industry is a great deal smaller than it once was, tourism has taken up the slack; in summer, Kalymnos is busy with holiday-making families from several European countries.

Kalymnos has a barren interior with dramatic cliffs and caves all around its coastline. The capital, **Pothia**, is a splash of bright colour climbing a hillside on the south coast. With a population of around 11,000, it is one of the largest towns in the Dodecanese and the major port on Kalymnos. Today, a small fleet of sponge fishermen still sets sail every summer, although the crop remains in decline. The statue of a mermaid sits on the breakwater as a lucky omen for the sailors, and families turn out to perform a religious ceremony to guide and protect their loved ones.

Beyond Pothia, the castle (Pera Kastro) at **Horio**, the medieval capital, is clearly visible. The beach resorts of **Mirties** and **Massouri** on the west coast take the bulk of visitors. Mirties is lush with vegetation, and palms, hibiscus and grape arbours adorn its buildings.

Massouri has fleets of boats that offer day trips to the island of **Telendos** only a mile or so offshore. Telendos was joined to Kalymnos until AD 554 when an earthquake tore the land apart. Buildings from a town that disappeared into the resulting channel are said to be visible in certain conditions. Today, a waterside hamlet with stylish tavernas lies at the foot of the island's **Mount Rahi**. On the outskirts of the settlement are the ruins of a Byzantine monastery and baths. The best beach is the pebbly **Hohlakas**, just to the west.

Returning to Kalymnos, if you continue north along the road from Pothia, you will come to the quieter villages of

Kalymnos built its reputation on sponge-fishing.

Aryinonda and **Emborio** with their rough pebble beaches. To the east of Pothia, the road leads to a fertile fruit-producing valley near **Vathi**. Offshore are the remains of an Italian naval vessel sunk by British forces in World War II.

Karpathos

This rugged and wild island lies between Rhodes and Crete, almost at the foot of the Aegean. Since the early 20th century, a large percentage of the population, tired of fighting the hard economic conditions, emigrated to the United States.

The remaining population of **Karpathos** is based mainly in the south of the island, around the capital, **Pigadia**, which is relatively modern by Greek standards (built since the mid-19th century). Around it lie fields of fertile soil, which support orchards and grain crops.

For centuries, the village of Olymbos was almost totally isolated from the rest of Karpathos, with the road from the south of the island – incredibly – only being completed in 1979.

The middle of the island has mountains that rise to more than 1,200 m (4,050 ft), protecting the north of the island from the effects of development in the south. From Pigadia to the small southern port of **Diafani**, where vehicles find it hard to travel, boats move people and goods. From here it is a steep journey up to the village of **Olymbos**, which still holds fast to its traditional way of life. Houses here are built to a long-standing design and filled with embroidery, lace and crochet work. Older women in the village still dress in colourful traditional costumes, which the younger women and children wear on feast days.

The remaining parts of the north, although enticing, are rather difficult to explore. One exception to this is the hike

On festival day the women of Karpathos dress in traditional costume.

north from Olymbos to the shrine to St John the Baptist at
Vrykounda, site of a major island festival on 29 August
every year.

THE EASTERN AEGEAN

Close to western Turkey, three large islands lie aligned from
north to south: Lesvos, Chios and Samos. These islands,
known as the eastern Aegean Islands, have been at the fore-
front of waves of invasion from the east. Phoenicians and
Persians came here to attack the kingdoms of the ancient
Greek mainland; later, the Ottomans used this region as a
base when they forced the Venetians and the Genoese to flee
back to their homelands. The populations of all three islands
played a major role in the fight for Greek statehood at the beginning of the 19th century. They also saw a wave of Greek
immigrants from the Turkish mainland during and after the
proclamation of the Turkish state in 1923.

Despite hostile feelings existing in the past, relations between Greece and Turkey are now rather more genial, at least on a day-to-day basis. One of the most exciting facets of a trip to the eastern Aegean Islands is the possibility of taking a day trip to Turkey, where you can experience the contrasting (though sometimes surprisingly similar) culture, and see some of the majestic ancient archaeological sites of old Asia Minor.

Lesvos

The third-largest Aegean island (after Crete and Evia), **Lesvos**, has a long and independent cultural tradition. Music, poetry and dance have always been important aspects of the island's identity. It was the birthplace of the ancient poet Sappho, said by Homer to be the tenth muse, and the musician Alcaeus, the father of Greek music. The Ottoman Sultans held Lesvos in high esteem for its fertile lands and the fine olive oil produced here; after the creation of the Turkish state in the 1920s, however, Lesvos lost its main market and became a backwater of the Aegean.

The island's capital is **Mytilini** (you may sometimes hear Greeks call the island Mytilini, rather than Lesvos). A trading town and port, its main shopping street, **Ormos Ermou**, still throngs with the energy of an eastern bazaar. Fine 18th-century villas can be found along the seafront, both north of the port and south towards the airport. The villas were built for Ottoman traders and overseers, but were abandoned in the exchange of populations in the 1920s.

> It is claimed that the best olive oil in Greece is produced on Lesvos. The olives are harvested in November and December and pressed within 24 hours of being picked.

The most impressive structure is the **medieval castle** built atop Roman, Hellenistic, and more ancient settlements. One of the biggest fortifications in the Aegean, the interior Venetian walls were later expanded by the Ottomans. Resting in the shadow of the castle walls is the **Lesvos Archaeological Museum**, home to one of the finest collections of artefacts in Greece. An air-conditioned, state-of-the-art building has been added on to the original museum, a fine old mansion. Throughout the two structures there are finds from all eras of Lesvos's history. Intricate mosaics depicting scenes from Menender's

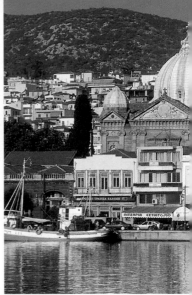

Mytileni, the capital of Lesvos, has a modern, busy port.

comedies are exhibited beautifully, with clear glass tile walkways allowing close access to the detail. Greek and Roman statuary, jewellery and daily utensils are all thoughtfully arranged on display.

Around the island, Lesvos offers wonderful impressions of Greek village life. Its economy depends far less on tourist earnings and much more on agricultural production (re-established since the problems of the 1920s); therefore, traditional lifestyles are common here.

The east of the island has the majority of the estimated 10 million olive trees, which produce the island's major crop. They blanket the hills with their silvery leaves,

The remains of an impressive Roman aqueduct at Moria.

shimmering in the breeze. Small villages (built inland to offer protection against marauding pirates) with narrow cobbled streets sit among them.

North of Mytilini, stop at the village of **Moria**. Here, you will find the remains of a huge Roman aqueduct that are usually surrounded by grazing goats.

Mandamadhos village in the far north of Lesvos still carries on a traditional pottery industry, albeit on a small scale. On its outskirts, the **Monastery of Taxiarhis** is home to a revered black icon that is believed to be fashioned from soil wet with the blood of monks slaughtered at the abbey.

Continue along this road to reach the pretty coastal town of **Molyvos** – also known by its ancient name of Mithymna – a popular spot for tourists. The medieval streets and Ottoman houses have been transformed into galleries and cafés, and a small castle sits proudly above the town. The harbour sheltered below the castle offers an ideal place to enjoy lunch.

South of Molyvos, the resort town of **Petra** has an 18th-century townhouse museum and a pretty church built on a large rock at its centre. The northwest area offers a complete contrast to the olive groves of the east, with a volcanic landscape totally devoid of trees. The **Monastery of Ipsilou** sits in this minimalist panorama, reaching up towards the sky as if for inspiration.

Located just west of the monastery lies one of the geological wonders of the world. In ancient times, this land had a forest of giant sequoia trees. Volcanic ash covered some of the trees while they were still alive and over time their trunks turned to stone. Now known as the **Petrified Forest**, a number of these trees can be seen, some with every growth ring visible. To the southwest of the Petrified Forest, take the road to Eressos and its beach resort of **Skala Eressos**, birthplace of the poet Sappho.

The southern coastline is divided by the large inlet of Kolpos Kallonis, but beyond this, in the south of the island, the olive is king, especially around **Mount Olymbos**, the highest point on Lesvos. **Aghiasos** village lies in its shadow. A traditional settlement, Aghiasos holds a major festival at its **Panagia Vrefokratoussa** church on 15 August every year. **Plomari** on the south coast is a centre for fine ouzo production, and both Plomari and neighbouring **Vatara** have good beaches, now being developed for tourism. From Lesvos, there are regular summer excursions to the Turkish coastal town of **Ayvilik**, a base for trips to the sites of ancient Troy and Pergamum.

Sappho of Lesvos

Born in 612 BC on Lesvos, Sappho and her family were exiled to Sicily during her childhood, but later she returned to the island to marry and bear a child. Sappho is renowned for her poems, which speak of love and tenderness and are written in a form now known as 'Sapphic stanzas'. The poet created a commune of women at ancient Eressos, which promoted the natural bonds of sorority. Her work, along with her social activities, led her to become a torchbearer for homosexual women, and the word 'lesbian' is taken from the island of her birth (the letter 'b' is pronounced as a 'v' in Greek).

Chios

On arrival at the port of **Chios Town**, it is tempting to pass through quickly, for it offers a dreary welcome to the island. However, Chios island (also known as Hios) has some very beautiful secrets to reveal to those who venture further.

> **Chios is renowned for its mastic production. The Romans made toothpicks from the gum; in Istanbul the sultan's concubines used it to freshen their breath; and Hippocrates praised its therapeutic value for treating coughs and colds.**

During the 14th century, Chios enjoyed a period of wealth and stability under the Genoese. When the Ottomans took control in 1566, they continued to allow the population privileges unknown on other islands. In part, this related to the gum mastic produced here (a rare and valuable commodity, highly prized for its use in medicine). However, the population of Chios has also experienced very turbulent times, particularly in 1822, when an estimated 20,000 people were massacred by Ottoman forces, following an unsuccessful uprising against Ottoman rule just after the creation of the Greek state in 1821.

Behind its concrete façade (a result of rebuilding after numerous earthquakes), Chios Town has a number of clues to its past. Remnants of a **medieval kastro** and a fine **archaeological museum** housed in a mosque are two of the highlights. There is also the splendid **Argenti Museum and Korai Library** on Odos Korai Street, with its collection of costumes and folk art dating from 2,000 years ago.

Out in the countryside, Chios has other attractions to offer. Travel south from Chios Town to reach the mastic groves. Collecting and processing the crop is still a profitable industry. Look out for a number of fine Italian mansions in the plains around **Kambos**. Many are still in private hands.

The 20 mastic villages, known collectively as *mastihohoria*, were built by the Genoese in the 14th and 15th centuries. Their intricate and confusing maze of narrow alleyways was deliberately created to confound invaders. They now often do the same to strolling visitors. Most of the villages remain virtually unchanged since their creation – save for a plethora of TV antennae – and offer a fascinating view of Greek village life, where tomatoes hang from every window and the elderly inhabitants discuss the day's news on their doorsteps.

Pyrgi village, with its walls marked by the incised black-and-white geometric pattern known as *xysta*, is probably the most popular with tourists, although **Mesta** is also beautiful and worth a visit. After your explorations, head towards the coast and the black pebble beach of **Emborio** to enjoy a cooling dip in the sea.

Houses on Chios decorated in traditional *xysta* patterns.

To the west of Chios Town is a graphic reminder of a bloodbath that took place in 1822. High on a rocky bluff is the village of **Anavatos**, which lost a large percentage of its population in a massacre – its women and children chose suicide rather than the Ottoman sword and threw themselves from the rocky precipice at the top of the village. Wander along the empty streets to take in the sombre atmosphere of the place.

The Monastery of Néa Moni has seen its share of turmoil.

Located just nearby is the **Monastery of Nea Moni**, which was founded in 1049 and is one of the most beautiful Byzantine religious sites in the Aegean. The monastery rests in a fertile valley and is surrounded by plane and pine trees. Mosaics inside a small chapel are of the finest quality and show scenes of the life of Christ. The monastery also suffered damage in 1822. Its more portable treasures were stolen, but a lasting memorial to the massacre is an ossuary, or depository for the bones of the dead. In spite of this gruesome reminder, the site is perfect for quiet reflection, and is tended now by a couple of elderly nuns. Beyond Anavatos and Nea Moni are wonderful beaches around the coastal town of **Volissos**, where you will find a quiet place to acquire (or burnish) your suntan.

Samos

A fertile island of vines, olive groves and pine forest, just 3 km (2 miles) from the Turkish coast, **Samos** has taken a back seat in Aegean history since its golden age in the fifth century BC. Today it is growing in popularity with tourists, and resort facilities are expanding.

The main town, **Vathi** – also known as Samos Town – lies on the northeastern coastline in a very sheltered harbour. It has few facilities for tourists, but the atmosphere is friendly and there's a good **archaeological museum** that exhibits a giant *kouros* 5 m (16 ft) high. **Ano Vathi** – an older town – sits on the hillside behind and is now bypassed by the new road system.

The much smaller town of **Pithagorio** on the southeastern coast is the site of the ancient capital. It was a centre of power in the 17th century BC, when the Samians were the leading maritime nation on the Aegean. In 538 BC, power fell into the hands of Polycrates, a ruthless but brilliant leader. He accumulated untold wealth through trade and piracy, funding an extensive construction programme and a court that attracted such luminaries as the storyteller Aesop and the mathematician Pythagoras (a local Samian, who later fled the island to escape Polycrates's cruelty). Following the death of Polycrates, Samos was plunged into a sudden and deep decline.

The remains of the Temple of Hera on Samos.

Pithagorio has a very pretty harbour and the ruins of a Frankish castle. The only evidence of Polycrates's time is the giant mole, which, now strengthened, still stands on the ancient foundations. Two more massive projects can be found in the surrounding countryside. To the west, beyond the airport, are the remains of the **Temple of Hera**, or the Heraion. It would have been the largest temple in the world at the time, but it was never completed. In the hills above Pithagorio is perhaps the most amazing example of Polycrates' wealth and power. He funded the cutting of a tunnel more than 1,000 m (3,333 ft) long to bring water to the ancient capital. The **Tunnel of Eupalinos** can be explored but it's not for the claustrophobic.

On the northern coast, the village of **Kokari** has a picturesque harbour and is a strong magnet for visitors. Small villages in the interior remain unspoiled, particularly because of their remote and hilly location. Among the prettiest is **Marathokambos**, nestling in the shadow of **Mount Kerkis**. The beaches of Samos provide some of the best conditions for windsurfing in the Aegean, particularly on the western coast. From Samos, it is only a short ferry trip east to the Turkish port of **Kusadasi** and the site of ancient **Ephesus**.

THE NORTHERN AEGEAN

Like Lesvos, Chios and Samos, the islands of the northern Aegean have been influenced by their proximity to the Turkish coastline, with Limnos in particular playing an important strategic role on shipping lanes to and from the Dardanelles.

The islands also lie close to the northern Greek mainland and the Balkans region, giving their history altogether different influences than that of their neighbours further south in the Aegean.

Thassos

This small, round tree-covered island is a favourite holiday spot for families from the cities of northern Greece, being only 12 km (8 miles) from the coastline of Macedonia. It has until recently seen fewer foreign visitors, although package flights from Europe now land at the airport of **Kavala** on the mainland for the short ferry crossing. In ancient times,

Not without reason, Thassos is renowned for its beautiful beaches.

Thassos was renowned for its sweet white wine, but today its beaches are the major draw. They are considered some of the most beautiful in the Aegean.

The capital, **Thassos Town**, also known as **Limin**, is a modern port built on the site of a medieval fortress and a classical Greek settlement. Large areas of the site have been excavated and the **archaeological museum** houses a comprehensive collection of finds. There are a number of individual buildings to explore. They include a **shrine to Pan** built on a rocky outcrop and the **Gate of Parmenon**, reached by way of a steep run of steps – the last remaining ancient port of entry to the town.

Beyond Limin, Thassos is mountainous and covered with pine forest. Tourism has spread throughout the island, but does not overpower its natural charms. The island is renowned for its nuts, honey and fruits, which traditionally have been preserved to last through the Aegean winters. The closest resort to the capital is **Makriamos**. Hotels and tavernas also border the fine beaches at **Krissi Amoudia** and **Skala Potamias**.

Inland settlements offer fascinating insights into life in bygone ages. **Theologos** was the Ottoman capital of Thassos, and has many preserved mansions. Even higher up in the mountains, **Kastro** was built to evade the attention of marauding pirates, and still proves elusive to all but the most determined visitors.

Limnos

Limnos lies closest to the Dardanelles, and for this reason the island is dominated by the Greek military, which keeps a watchful eye on activity through the straits. It has long been a military station for the dominant nation of the area, and was a major staging point for British and Commonwealth troops before the fated Gallipoli campaign of World War I. A cemetery for 900 of these gallant men can be found at **Moudros**, near the harbour where they set forth to their fate.

The capital of the island is **Myrina**. Small stone houses crowd the town centre with fine Ottoman houses along the northern edge of town. A small archaeological museum dis-

---

The Mysteries of the Underworld

The Great Gods of Samothraki were of Balkan and Anatolian origin. They included Axieros, the Great Mother figure, represented in sculpture on sacred rocks with her companion, Kadmilos. Two other Gods, Axiokersos and Axiokersa (in some ways equivalents of the Greek God of Hell, Hades, and his wife Persephone) were condemned to remain in the Underworld – a place of moral judgement similar to the purgatory of Catholic belief.

plays finds from the island, including the eastern site of **Polyohni**, which was a thriving city before its destruction by earthquake in 2100 BC. The remains of the Byzantine kastro can also be explored. The coastline north and south of Myrina has some fine stretches of sandy beach, and there is a small resort at **Akti Myrina**. Unfortunately, poor roads and limited public transport hinder exploration of other parts of the island.

In ancient times, Samothraki was an important centre of culture.

Samothraki

A series of rocky cliffs line the shoreline of Samothraki which, unlike other islands, has poor natural anchorages. Inland, **Mount Fengari**, the Aegean's highest peak at 1,610 m (5,000 ft), dominates the landscape. It was from here, according to Homer, that the God Poseidon watched the Battle of Troy taking place, looking east across the water. The capital, **Chora Town**, is a classic example of a settlement built out of sight of pirate forces. It nestles in a valley 5 km (3 miles) inland, unseen by passing ships.

Today, the island is little more than a forgotten backwater with few ferry connections to other islands, but its strong natural defences gave it advantages in ancient times. Until the advent of Christianity, Samothraki was a very important island indeed.

From the late Bronze Age, a centre of religious worship developed on the northern coast, which was later dedicated to Castor and Pollux, the patron saints of sailors. It was also home to the powerful Cult of the Underworld. Many, including Philip of Macedon, father of Alexander the Great, travelled here to be initiated into its inner circle.

The remains of the centre, the **Sanctuary of the Great Gods** near the town of **Paleopoli**, now form one of the major archaeological sites in the eastern Aegean. The site ruins, mostly from the Hellenistic period, lie almost overgrown, but they are perfect for exploring at your own pace.

Highlights include the **Arsinoion rotunda** built for Egyptian Queen Arsinoe in the third century BC from marble brought from Thassos. At the time it was the largest circular building in the world, measuring 20 m (65 ft) in diameter. In 1863, on a hill above the theatre, a French diplomat discovered the statue of the **Winged Victory of Samothraki**. The original statue, dating from the fourth century BC, is in the Louvre in Paris.

The more modest museum at the site has many finds, including a fine carved Temenos frieze (fourth century BC) of musicians and dancing girls.

Therma on the north coast is still an active spa offering treatments for ailments from rheumatism to infertility. It is also the starting point for three-hour treks to the summit of **Mount Fengari**, where you can clearly see the Turkish coast – just as Poseidon did.

THE SPORADES

Sporades means scattered, and this group of four islands lies off the Greek mainland in just this fashion. Part of Greece from the moment of statehood, the Sporades islands see many Greek mainland visitors, and were once the exclusive domain of an independent sailing fraternity. Today, a rental fleet makes it possible for almost anyone to enjoy a sail in this dreamy place.

Skiathos

This is the smallest of the main Sporades islands and it lies closest to the Greek mainland. **Skiathos Town**, the only settlement on the island, is a bustling resort, rebuilt after severe damage in World War II. Urbane Athenians spend summer weekends here, rubbing shoulders with the foreign tourists who crowd the bars and clubs. A fleet of sailing boats for hire uses this port as a base, and commercial ferries ply their regular routes to other islands from here.

The commercial ferry port is separated from the picturesque fishing harbour by Bourdzi islet, where you can sit under pine trees and admire the view. The small fort built on the islet now hosts open-air concerts in the summer months. A series of restaurants lines the harbourside and the narrow cobbled streets behind. Numerous small boutiques make the old town a good place for souvenir hunt-

Skiathos Town spreads out along the island's steeply sided coast.

ing. However, the lure of Skiathos has always been its beaches – more than 60 of them edge its 44-km (27-mile) coastline. A regular bus service runs along the southern shore, terminating at perhaps the most famous, **Koukounaries Beach**. A long arc of fine sand backed by pine trees, Koukounaries is perhaps the epitome of everything that beach-lovers enjoy. Shallow waters, sports and refreshments add to the fun. Perhaps the only problem is that you will be fighting for space on the sand with just about every other tourist on the island. A short walk over the hill brings you to **Krassi Beach**, a nudists' beach appropriately renamed **Banana Beach** by the locals.

Beaches along the northern shore are better reached by caique (a small, brightly painted ferry). **Lalaria Beach** is among the most beautiful, with cliffs and natural arches flanking the pebbled bay. The boat trip will also take you past **Kastro**, the long abandoned 16th-century capital. Now in ruins, it sits atop a rocky promontory.

Skopelos

The population of Skopelos is renowned for its friendliness and hospitality, and the natural beauty of the island is equally inviting. **Skopelos Town** is one of the most impressive towns of its size in the Aegean, in part because it is also among the most original – little damaged either by war or earthquakes. Its grey-tiled roofs cascade down a hill in the shape of an amphitheatre towards the tiny port. Round church towers topped with tiny crosses punctuate the skyline. The ruined Venetian castle atop a small hill offers panoramic views over the whole town, while the roof of the particularly beautiful **Church of Christ** along the harbour stands out from the open sea.

The interior of the island is a wonderful mixture of mountainous dark pine forest and farmland. There are fewer

The Chuch of Christ forms a prominent landmark on Skopelos.

beaches than on other islands in the Sporades, but yachts
moor in the numerous rocky inlets around the coastline where
there is excellent snorkelling and swimming. **Panormos** and
Agnondas on the south coast attract tourists, as does **Stafy-
los Beach**, where the tomb of an ancient king of the same
name was found in 1927.

Alonissos

The island of **Alonissos** has been settled longer than any
other in the Aegean and is estimated by archaeologists to
date from 100,000 BC. It was highly esteemed by many
leaders in classical Greek times but in the 20th century
suffered a number of severe setbacks that made it a backwater of the Aegean – until fairly recently, that is. The wine
produced on the island was prized for many centuries, but a
bout of Phylloxera disease killed the vines, and in 1965 a
large earthquake destroyed the island's major settlement.

Nowadays, the majority of people visit Alonissos for its natural beauty. Much of the sea around the island has been designated as a marine conservation area called the **Sporades Marine Park**, which includes several small islands offshore. This protects a population of monk seals and other marine life, as well as archaeological remains on the seabed.

Palea Alonissos, which was destroyed in the earthquake of 1965, is just a five-minute bus ride inland from the port of **Patitiri**, and its old houses are slowly being restored with outside investment. Views from its Byzantine walls are spectacular. The road network is limited, but there is a bus service to the **Kokkinokastro Peninsula** where the most popular beaches lie. Fleets of small caiques travel to more remote beaches that lie all around the coastline.

> Since ancient times, the inhabitants of Skyros have bred a unique strain of dwarf pony (about the size of a Shetland pony) that is thought to be descended from the ancient Pikermic breed. The tiny horses represented on the frieze of the Parthenon in Athens are probably Skyros ponies.

Skyros

The largest and most remote island in the Sporades – a two-hour ferry journey southeast of Skiathos – – **Skyros** has been little affected by tourism. It is a mountainous island and its inhabitants have a rugged individuality that matches the landscape. The whole island takes part in the **Skyros Carnival**, an annual event that is held in the days leading up to Lent. Grotesque animal costumes are worn, bawdy jokes are exchanged, and ritual dances are performed.

The main settlement on the island, **Skyros Town**, on the east coast, is topped with a **Byzantine/Venetian kastro**. Legend says that Theseus was thrown to his death here, many generations ago. In the north of the town, a local artist, Manos Faltaïts, has developed a museum of Skyrian folklore and tradition. The **Faltaïts Museum** is housed in an old mansion and features costumes, arts and crafts, and photographs. There is also an **archaeological museum** that displays older relics, including examples of Mycenaean pottery. To the north is the long, sandy **Magazia Beach**.

The south of the island is mountainous and barren and travelling there is difficult. British poet **Rupert Brooke** is buried at **Tris Boukes**, a bay in the far south. He died in 1915 while on his way to fight in the Dardanelles during World War I.

To the north, wooded hillsides and olive groves surround the airport. Ferries arrive at **Linaria** on the east coast, and in pastures around the village it is possible to see the last examples of the famed Skyrian miniature horses *(see box left)*.

The houses of Skyros Town tumble down towards the sea.

WHAT TO DO

Island life is certainly relaxing, and in the Aegean there is no pressure on visitors to do anything. However, for those with the energy, there's plenty to do.

BEACHES

Beaches come in all sizes, from the tiny cove where you can spend the day alone, to wide sandy bays where you can be sure of the company of hundreds. Some have ample shade and others are treeless, catering to ardent sun worshippers. Many people decry the pebble beach, preferring soft sand; however, in the summer Meltemi winds, pebbles of coin size don't blow around and spoil your day, whereas sand does. Santorini has volcanic sand in both black and red, which absorbs heat much more readily than yellow sand and therefore becomes much hotter in the heat of the day – not good for small children who want to run around and play. For fine sand beaches, you the best advised to visit Koukanaries on Skiathos, Golden on Paros, and Paradise on Mykonos. There's also Milopotamos on Ios and Makriamos on Thassos.

In Europe in the 1960s, the Greek islands became known for their laid-back attitude towards visitors. Naturists flocked to the area. Although things have changed a little today, there are still nude beaches on some of the islands, notably Paradise and Super-Paradise on Mykonos and Banana Beach on Skiathos. However, on most islands, nudity is not official policy, and clothing will certainly not be optional on beaches that are popular with families. If you want to be sure of not catching sight of anything risqué, follow the local people.

Panormos beach on Skopelos, a little corner of paradise.

SPORTS

You'll find a wide range of watersports on offer on the Aegean Islands. Jetskiing is popular almost everywhere, while windsurfing is best where the prevailing winds and wide sandy bays allow the sail to catch the breeze. Conditions are particularly strong on the west coast of Paros, where the World Windsurfing Championships are held every year. You can also find good offshore conditions at Naxos, Samos and Kos.

Many beaches also have water rides in which you sit on or in a rubber shape and are pulled along behind a speed boat.

Perfect conditions for windsurfing in the Aegean

Diving

Although the warm, clear waters of the Aegean constitute a near-perfect diving environment, until recently the Greek government was rightly concerned about the possible damage divers might do to submerged ancient sites, and diving was prohibited. However, attitudes have changed, and diving is now a legal and welcomed activity, provided you dive with an approved and registered organisation. A number of companies are already operating on islands. They supervise dives and provide transport to the sites. Each dive centre is registered by the Greek government, and qualified to offer training for novice divers and supervision for qualified divers. All centres are affiliated with one of the major certifying bodies, PADI (Professional Association of Diving Instructors) being the most common. The basic qualification, the Open Water certificate, takes five days to complete. On completion, you will be allowed to dive with an instructor to a depth of 18 m (60 ft). This enables you to experience many dive sites

A diving platform acts as a base for underwater expeditions.

in the Aegean Sea. Many centres also offer an introductory session commonly known as the Discover Scuba programme. This involves a half-day of theory and shallow-water work, giving you an opportunity to try out the basic techniques before committing yourself a full course.

Mykonos has had a head start as far as diving is concerned because it was never banned here (no ancient sites to protect). Dive Adventures at Paradise Beach (Tel. 02890 26539 in season; Tel. 010 7560552 during the winter) is an established centre. Santorini also has interesting dive sites. You can discover the sheer underwater walls in the caldera, or visit the reef off the eastern coast. Contact Mediterranean Dive Club at Perissa Beach (Tel. 02860 83080 in season; Tel. 010 4125376 during the winter).

Paros has cave, reef and wreck diving around its shores, giving the diver a wide range of environments to explore. Several dive centres operate on the island, including Santa

Maria Diving Club at Naoussa on the northern coast (Tel. 02840 385307; fax 02840 53007). Kos has some well-organised dive operators at its resorts. Contact Theokritos Travel (Tel. 02420 69666; fax 02420 69112).

Sailing

With its centuries-old seafaring tradition, the Aegean has long been attractive to sports sailors. Many of the elite of Athens have sailed the short distance from the capital for a weekend at a deserted inlet. Until recently, there was little for those who lacked a yacht, but now there are sailing fleets waiting to be hired either with or without a crew. Flotillas can be organised for gregarious island-hopping or you can wend your own way at your own pace. The largest hire fleets are found in Athens, Skiathos or on Kos. Contact Sunsail, a UK-based company (Tel. 44 (0)1705 222222; fax 44 (0)1705 219827; web site <www.sunsail.com>) for further details.

Snorkelling

You can rent or buy snorkelling equipment in all the major resorts, allowing you to explore the beach shallows and rocky inlets. You'll see shoals of fish, sea urchins and even small octopuses that make their homes in rocky crevices.

Walking and Hiking

Exploring the coastline or interior of the Greek islands offers a different experience with each season of year. In late spring the hillsides are awash with flowers, and crops such as corn give the fields a golden hue. As summer progresses and the crops are harvested (usually early July), the ground dries and becomes dustier. The distinctive sound of the cicada chirps through the heat of the day. In autumn, the earth gives back the heat it absorbed during the summer, as the air begins to cool. Spring and autumn offer the clearest air for panoramic views of the surrounding land; in summer, a heat-induced haze rises, cutting long-distance visibility.

There are some interesting, though not too difficult hikes on the islands. Don't forget to take a supply of water and wear sturdy footwear. If you walk in summer, early morning or late afternoon is best.

On Santorini, there is a footpath along the lip of the caldera which leads from the town of Fira to Ia, offering stunning views of the whole area. On Paros, the marble-clad Byzantine road at Lefkes takes you down the valley to Karampoli. There are hundreds of old donkey trails to explore on Tinos. On Karpathos, you can walk from the traditional settlement of Olymbos to the shrine of St John in the north of the island.

On Samothraki, it is possible to climb to the summit of Mount Fengari, where the God Poseidon watched the Trojan

The foothills of Mount Zas, a popular place for walking on Naxos.

War reach its tragic climax. On Naxos, you can walk through the pretty villages of the Tragea Valley and the foothills of Mount Zas, admiring Byzantine churches and exploring olive groves at your leisure.

SHOPPING

The maze of narrow streets that comprise many old towns in the Aegean are home to a fascinating mixture of art and sculpture galleries, jewellery and clothes shops and stores selling collectables. It's possible to spend hours browsing for the perfect souvenir.

Antiques

For serious collectors, there are genuine antiques for sale throughout the Aegean (anything made or produced before 1821 is officially classified as an antique), in the form of sculpture, pottery, or icons. Any antiques will require proper accreditation, and in some cases a permit, if they are to be exported from the country. The antiques dealer should be able to advise you in this process. For those whose budget won't stretch to the real thing, there are plenty of reproductions on offer. Quality and prices vary.

Island Specialities

Each island has its own speciality. On Kalymnos, you can buy wonderful natural sponges that have been collected at sea by island divers. Lesvos is known for its olive oil and ouzo, while Mykonos is reputed for its cotton jumpers. On Naxos, sample *kitron*, a lemon-based liqueur, and on Sifnos look out for its pottery, which is finely decorated with classical motifs. Thassos is known for its honey and delicious fruit jams, while on Tinos, you'll find marble from Pyrgos, incense and candles. The choice is yours.

Art and Sculpture

You'll notice that prices for articles that are based on the same design and may, at first glance, look the same, range from only a few euros to many thousands. This is because there is tremendous variation in the quality of the materials used and the skills involved. Look out for the weight of a piece of pottery or sculpture and the amount of detail in the decoration or the carving.

Traditional themes include Cycladic figures, or pottery with scenes taken from ancient Greek frescoes or mosaics.

Modern artists flock to the main islands, both to work

The price of bronzes and classical sculptures varies considerably.

and to sell their pieces. Often a village house will be transformed into a small and enticing gallery. The range of styles and media means that you are sure to find a souvenir that suites your taste.

Clothing

Traditional Greek clothing is little in evidence, but most of the islands have narrow lanes festooned with cool cotton or cheesecloth trousers, tops and dresses, all of which are ideal for the summer climate. You will also find the ubiquitous T-shirt in a variety of styles, along with swimwear and footwear. In fact, you may not even need to pack any clothes

Traditional white cotton pullovers for sale on Mykonos.

for your trip. Just buy them when you arrive.

Santorini and Mykonos in particular have a plethora of designer clothing and shoes from Europe and the United States. Many of the familiar names (Armani, DKNY) have their own air-conditioned boutiques. Traditional thick cotton sweaters can still be found on Mykonos (ideal for evening in the late season), although outlets are closing to make way for designer shops. Buy soon or you may miss the chance.

Food

The abundant fruit grown on the islands in the summer continues to be preserved to last through the cold winters. Cherries, plums and figs are made into jams. Bees harvest the pollen of the wild herbs on the hillsides to produce delicious honey to which fresh nuts (almonds or walnuts) are added. Olives are preserved in oil or brine, or you could simply take home a bottle of extra virgin olive oil both for cooking and to make salad dressings.

Jewellery

Precious stones glitter in shops on the streets of Mykonos and Santorini, and you can choose as many carats as your budget can handle. Gold and silver are sold by weight, with relatively little extra cost added for workmanship, making them a good buy. Ancient Greek designs are very much in evidence in gold, silver and non-precious metals. Favourite designs are Hellenic, Minoan and Macedonian.

At the other extreme, there are many forms of hippie jewellery from anklets in metal or leather to finger and toe rings.

Leatherware

Greek islanders have always worked the leather from their arable herds to make handbags, wallets, belts and footwear in a variety of styles and patterns, although it cannot match the quality of the Italian-produced leather products sold in boutiques in Santorini and Mykonos. However, prices for native-produced items are cheaper.

ENTERTAINMENT

Nightlife varies from island to island, and on some of the smaller islands, an evening will revolve around dinner and conversation at the local taverna, or a stroll along the seafront. However, traditional Greek dances and musical performances, as well as clubs with DJs spinning dance music can be found.

Music and Dance

For many, the image of Greek music and dance is inexorably linked to the film *Zorba the Greek*. Anthony Quinn performs the *syrtaki* dance (in fact, an amalgam of several different traditional dances) to the sound of the *bouzouki*, a stringed-guitar instrument that produces melodic, slightly metallic sounds. When played live, it has a haunting melody but taverna owners do have the irritating habit of playing it at high decibels through overloaded speakers.

This does a great disservice to the Greek musical tradition, which is rich and varied and goes back hundreds of years. Musical rhythms were traditionally matched to the complex cadences of the epic poetry of Greece. Because these rhythms differ from the four beats to a bar notation we are accustomed to in the West, Greek music sometimes can be difficult to follow.

Each region of Greece has its own particular songs and dances. The music of the southern islands has a traditional style called *nisiotika*, while in the northern Aegean, a style called *sandouri* prevails. Most islands have a *syrtos* dance, or steps performed in the round.

In the 1920s, the tempestuous time of Turkish liberation, these dances instantly became known as the classical styles.

Tavernas resound to the rhythms of Greek music bands.

Also at that time, a new style, *rembetiko*, was created. Many Greeks in Asia Minor were forced to leave their homes and brought an influence of eastern cadences with them. The themes found in *rembetiko* are those closest to the hearts of the common man: lost love, poverty, social division, and discrimination. It's no surprise to discover that it is the most popular form of Greek music heard on the radio today.

It is becoming more difficult to see performances on the islands. Cultural festivals are one opportunity, but the better way is at a wedding or feast day when the performances are set in their true context. Many islands will also have one venue for Greek night, an evening of culinary and cultural delights. While Greek night may strike some visitors as contrived, it is an opportunity to see a local art form.

Kos's ancient theatre, a venue for classical performances.

Ancient Greek Drama

Performances of classical Greek theatre take place on some islands. Although it is now performed in the modern rather than the classical Greek language, it is still not easy to understand, so try to find an English copy of the plot before the performance begins. When you see the plays performed in the ancient theatres of classical or Roman times, such as those on Thassos or Kos, it makes it all worthwhile. Sitting in the balmy evening air with only natural acoustics to aid the actor's delivery is a special experience.

Nightlife

For those who can't go on holiday without the chance of dancing to throbbing music well into the early hours of the morning, look no further than the towns of Fira on Santorini, Mykonos Town on Mykonos, Skiathos Town on Skiathos, or Chora on Ios. Here you can party to your heart's content.

ACTIVITIES FOR CHILDREN

Children are welcomed all over the Greek islands, and they will be fussed over and indulged in cafés and restaurants. Young children love beach activities, and as the Aegean has little tidal range and plenty of wide shallow bays, it has many places which are safe for paddling and swimming. Sandy beaches are more fun than pebbles for castle building and hole digging, so bear that in mind when choosing your island. Do remember that if you are taking young children to the beach the sun can be extremely hot. Keep young skins safe by covering them with sunblock or a T-shirt, even when in the water.

For older children, the range of water sports found in the popular resorts offers an exciting challenge. From pedal boats and canoes to windsurfing and jetskiing, the choice is yours. For even more fun, you could try the water park, Kolymithres, on Paros.

A Crusader castle brings swashbuckling to life, so try a trip to the walls of Mytilini or Kos Castle to become a knight of yore. *Caique* trips are popular, too. These small, prettily painted boats ply their routes from main towns to nearby beaches. Children love to watch the coastline go by, or point out shoals of small fish swimming in the clear water. As another activity, you could ride a donkey on Santorini from the port up to Fira town. Finally, visit the village of Olymbos on Karpathos, where the inhabitants, including children, wear elaborate and beautiful traditional costumes.

Children on Skopelos dressed for *Ochi* ('No' Day), 28 October.

Calendar of Events

There are more than 300 saints' days celebrated in the islands each year. Listed below is a selection of the main events and national celebrations shared with the Greek mainland.

1 January Known as *Protochronia*, but also called St Basil's Day, when prigs of basil are given as traditional gifts.

6 January Epiphany, when young men dive into the cold waters to recover a crucifix. Those who do are considered blessed for the year.

February/March Carnival time on many islands, particularly Skyros, Chios, Paros and Karpathos.

26 March Greek Independence Day featuring military parades.

Clean Monday First day of Orthodox Lent, marked by frugal meals. House cleaning and laundry also are undertaken with enthusiasm on this day.

Easter Easter is the most important of the Orthodox holidays. Candlelit processions follow a flower-decked bier on Good Friday. On Holy Saturday, a sacred flame is passed to each household to light a lamp of faith. On Sunday, lambs are sacrificed and roasted, signifying the start of another spring.

23 April St George's Day, a feast celebrating Greece's patron saint, with horse races and dancing on Limnos and Kos.

1 May May Day, marked by processions and flower festivals.

May Ceremony for the sponge fishermen on Kalymnos, as they head out to sea for another season's diving.

May/June Bull ceremonies on Lesvos.

17 July *Aghia Marina* coincides with the first grape crop.

15 August Assumption Day celebrates the reception of the Virgin Mary (*Panaghia*) into heaven. It is marked with processions on Tinos and Lesvos, and a festival on Paros. On Karpathos, women wear traditional dress for a colourful festival at the hillside town of Olymbos, which can last for days.

August Drama festival on Thassos; *Hippocratia* festival on Kos with a ceremony at the Asklepion.

26 October *Aghios Dhimitrios*, when the first wine is drunk.

28 October National *Ochi* ('No') Day, commemorating Greek defiance of the Italian invasion of 1940.

December Caroling in the days before Christmas and on New Year's Eve.

94

EATING OUT

Greek cuisine makes no pretence of emulating the classic cuisine of countries such as France, but it has always used local and often seasonal ingredients at their peak of flavour and freshness. Local people have relied on staples such as olive oil, wild herbs, seafood, lamb, or goat meat and an abundance of fresh vegetables, fruit and nuts since the islands were settled several millennia ago. Today, the Greek diet is one of the healthiest in the world, and its population is among the longest living. The extensive use of vegetables makes eating out a delight for vegetarians.

Mouthwatering watermelons for sale at an island market.

Over the centuries, the various cultures that have ruled the islands have left behind their own influences, which can still be experienced today. The Venetians and the Genoese, for example, left a legacy of tomato sauce that is used in many contemporary dishes; the Ottomans contributed yogurt, *souvlaki* (kebabs) and strong dark coffee.

Where to Eat

The Greek islands have a fascinating range of eateries that, at first glance, can be a little confusing for the visitor.

However, once you realise that, traditionally, Greek families never ate a three-course meal in one establishment, it brings the whole picture together. The appetiser and main course are eaten first, then one moves on to another place for sweets, and yet another for coffee. As tourist numbers grow, this system is gradually changing to the European or American custom of eating an entire meal in the same restaurant. However, on islands where traditions are strong, you will still find the following places to eat:

> You may be offered a sweet course in a taverna, only to see your waiter rushing off around the corner to return with your choice. In deference to a visitor's desire to have a full meal at one establishment, he has rushed to the local *zacharoplastia* (pastry shop) or *galaktopolio* (selling dairy dishes such as yogurt) to purchase a portion for you. The cost will be added to your bill.

The *ouzerie* is a traditional establishment selling not only the aniseed-flavoured alcoholic drink, *ouzo*, but also the *mezedes* dishes that accompany it (*ouzo* is never drunk on an empty stomach in Greece). The *mezedes* dishes can simply be a couple of appetisers or a full meal of several different small dishes. All will be absolutely fresh and delicious. Many *ouzeries* have octopuses hanging out to dry and tenderise. Octopus or squid is traditionally served with *ouzo*, but it is not compulsory. You will also have a range of hot and cold vegetable and meat dishes to choose from.

Visit the *psistaria* (the *gyro* and *souvlaki* shop). These most ancient of fast foods make tasty lunches or snacks. Later, peruse the amazing choices at the *zacharoplastia* (pastry shop) or the *galaktopolio*, which specialises in yogurt, cheese and other dairy dishes.

The *kafeneion* is the Greek coffee shop, traditionally the domain of the male, and it is still so in the inland villages on

islands such as Chios and Lesvos. Usually very plainly decorated, with a few old tables and chairs outside, it is a place of heated political debates and serious back-gammon games.

However, the taverna (you'll find it spelled *tabepna* on many Greek signs because 'b' is pronounced 'v' and 'p' is pronounced 'r' in the Greek language) is at the heart of Greek hospitality. It's where the appetiser and entrée courses have always been taken.

In the last few years, there has been a great move to cash in on the increase in the number of visitors and pass off frozen or mass-produced food as traditional home-cooked dishes. To find authentic cuisine, follow the local people. You may find yourself in some back street eatery away from the pretty views, but you can be sure that the food is excellent.

A sunny terrace outside a typical island taverna.

When to Eat

Many tavernas in the major resorts will be open to serve breakfast, lunch and dinner (breakfast includes a cooked English breakfast). However, traditionally, breakfast has been a small meal for Greeks (basically, a continental break-fast of bread, jam or honey and coffee.) Lunch is taken around 3pm, followed by a siesta before work begins again around 5.30pm. Dinner is taken late, usually around 10pm, though in summer tavernas will serve food as late as 1am.

Conversely, if you want to eat early, most tavernas will begin their evening service at around 6pm. You will definitely have your choice of table if you eat before 7.30pm, but restaurants will lack the colourful atmosphere of the later evening when local people come out to eat.

The Menu

In most traditional restaurants, you will be presented with an extensive menu, but not everything on it is available. Many foods are seasonal or made in batches (such as *moussaka*). Items currently available will have a price beside them.

Some of the best and most authentic restaurants will not even have a menu. The cook will prepare whatever is in season, and only a couple of dishes, to ensure that they are perfect. You simply go into the kitchen to see what looks and smells most enticing, then make your choice.

If the taverna has a barbecue, you will be invited to the grill to make your choice or to the ice table to choose your seafood. This is sold by weight, so always ask how much it will be before it is cooked to avoid a nasty surprise later.

All restaurants will levy a cover charge. This includes a serving of bread and is usually no more than €1 per person.

Appetisers

Greece is one country where appetisers can constitute a full meal. *Mezedes* (a selection of small appetiser dishes), shared by the whole table, offer a fun and relaxing way to eat. You simply have as little or as much as you want. As many are meatless, they are perfect for vegetarians, and waiters have no qualms about taking orders for an 'appetisers-only' meal.

The most popular *mezedes* are *tzatziki*, a yogurt dip flavoured with garlic, cucumber and mint; *dolmades*, vine leaves stuffed with rice and vegetables, which can be served hot or cold; and olives. There's *tarama*, cod-roe paste blended with breadcrumbs, olive oil and lemon juice; *fasolya*, beans in tomato sauce; and *kalamarakia tiganita*, pieces of deep-fried squid. *Tiropitikia*, small pastry parcels filled with cheese, are also common, along with *pastourma*, a kind of garlic sausage made with mutton or beef, and *keftedes*, small meatballs flavoured with coriander and spices. *Saganaki* is a slice of cheese coated in breadcrumbs and fried.

Greek salad or *horiatika* (literally translated as 'village salad') is tomato, cucumber, onion and olives topped with feta cheese, and can be taken as a meal in itself. When adding salad dressing (bottles of olive oil and wine vinegar are found with other condiments on the table), always add vinegar to the salad first, followed by oil.

Soups are staples of the Greek diet in winter, but their availability is more limited in summer. Fish soup is a standard on many menus. *Avgolemono*, a chicken broth with egg, lemon and rice, is delicious, but less commonly found. An Easter soup is *magaritsa*, made with lamb tripe, egg, lemon and lettuce. Traditionally, it is eaten to break the Lenten fast. *Revythia soupa* is a thick, chick-pea offering especially enjoyed on Sifnos.

Fish

With all the pretty harbours full of boats in the Aegean, it's no surprise that seafood forms a major part of the diet for islanders. You will find the day's catch on ice outside a taverna. The waiter will ask you to make your choice, which will be weighed and priced before cooking. Seafood is always a relatively expensive option by Greek standards, because of over-fishing in the surrounding seas. The most common fish are *barbounia* (red mullet), *xifias* (swordfish), and *lithrini* (bream). Seafood is always best served simply, and it is often

Octopuses drying in the sun – a familiar scene in the Cyclades.

grilled with fresh lemon. *Marides* (little fish or whitebait) is served fried, but you can find seafood served with white wine sauce, or sauces mixed with feta cheese.

Meat

Wherever you look, you will see barbecued meats. Fast foods include *gyros* (thin slices of meat cut from a spit and served with salad on pitta bread) or *souvlaki* (small chunks of meat on a skewer, also known by the Turkish name kebab). Barbecued dishes may include whole chickens, sides of lamb and veal, or stuffed loin of pork, all cooked to perfection. *Brizole* is a basic steak, but it may automatically come *bien cuit* (rare), rather than *à point* (well done). Roasted or barbecued lamb is the traditional Easter fare.

These dishes are easy to identify and order, but there are many superb slow-cooked oven dishes and stews, which are well worth trying. *Kleftiko* is braised lamb with tomatoes;

> Service is relaxed in Greek tavernas. Greeks view eating as a social occasion, not just a method of taking in calories. They're happy to sit and chat between courses and watch the world go by.

stifado is braised beef with onions. Each comes in an earthenware pot that keeps the contents piping hot.

Greece's most famous dish is probably *moussaka*, layers of aubergine and minced lamb with onions topped with béchamel sauce. At its best, it should be firm but succulent and aromatic with herbs. Good restaurants will make a fresh batch daily. Once it is gone, you'll have to wait until tomorrow. *Pastitsio* is another layered dish, this time of pasta (macaroni), meat and tomato sauce, originating in the Italian period in the history of the Aegean.

The northern islands have *kouneli* (rabbit) and *perdikes* (partridge), traditionally served sautéed. For those who want a hot meatless dish, there's *yemitsa*: tomatoes, aubergines, or peppers stuffed with a delicious rice and vegetable mixture.

Dessert

Most tavernas will bring a plate of fresh fruit as a finale to your meal. Often it is melon, or perhaps fresh figs. The *zacharoplastia* is the place to go for a full selection of desserts. Here you will find *baklava* (honey-soaked flaky pastry with walnuts), *katiafi* (shredded wheat filled with chopped almonds and honey) or *pita me meli* (honey cake). If you prefer dairy desserts, try delicious Greek yogurt with honey or fruit or *galaktobouriki* (custard pie).

Drinks

Dionysos, the God of Wine, made his home on Naxos, but in classical times, many more Greek islands produced wine. For centuries it was a major industry. Today, though the vintages aren't of French quality, there are some excellent producers and a good range to choose from. You will also find that a number of wines produced on the Greek mainland are imported to the islands.

Another option is to order wine from the barrel. This basic village wine will be served young and cool. Greece also produces a wine flavoured with resin called *retsina* (particularly useful in ancient times, because it kept the wine fresh in the hot climate). *Retsina* goes well with the Greek diet and the hot climate, but it is an acquired taste.

Ouzo is another drink that suits the hot climate. Taken as an aperitif, neat, or with ice and water, the aniseed flavour seems to cool the blood. However, don't overdo it as too much can result in a mighty hangover.

Those who prefer beer can find Amstel and Heineken brewed under licence on the Greek mainland. *Mythos* is a native Hellenic beer, which has a very crisp taste.

Some of the islands, notably Santorini, produce good wines.

Non-Alcoholic Drinks

Greece has fallen in love with the *café frappe* (strong cold coffee on ice). It's especially refreshing in the heat of the day. Hot coffee is made *ellenikos* or Greek style (indistinguishable from Turkish coffee). It's always freshly brewed in individual copper pots and served in small cups. It will automatically arrive *glykivastro* (very sweet) unless you order *metrio* (medium) or *sketo* (without sugar). Those who prefer instant coffee can order a drink known simply by its trade name, Nescafé or *nes*.

To Help You Order…

The following words and phrases should help you when ordering food and drink. You may want to purchase a copy of the *European Menu Reader* or the *Greek Phrase Book and Dictionary*. Both have a comprehensive glossary of Greek wining and dining.

I'd like a/an/some…   **Tha íthela…**
Could we have a table?   **Tha boroúsame na échoume éna trapézi?**

napkin	**trapezo-mándillo**	honey	**méli**
cutlery	**machero-pírouna**	water	**neró**
glass	**potíri**	egg	**avgó**
one	**éna/mia**	beef	**vodinó**
two	**dhío**	pork	**kirinó**
three	**tris/tría**	chicken	**kotópoulo**
four	**tésera**	prawns	**garída**
bread	**psomí**	octopus	**ktapódi**
wine	**krasí**	aubergine	**melitsána**
beer	**bíra**	(eggplant)	
fish	**psarí**	garlic	**skórdo**
fruit	**froúta**	ice cream	**pagotó**
meat	**kréas**	olives	**elyés**
milk	**gála**	lamb	**arní**
sugar	**záchari**	roasted or grilled	**psitó**
salt	**aláti**	butter	**vūtiro**
pepper	**pipéri**	chick peas	**revíthya**

HANDY TRAVEL TIPS

A

ACCOMMODATION (see CAMPING, YOUTH HOSTELS, and the list of RECOMMENDED HOTELS starting on page 128)

Hotels are divided into six classes: Luxury, A, B, C, D and E. Room rates for all categories except luxury are set by the Greek government. The classes are dictated by the facilities at the hotel, not the quality of the rooms. This means that a class C hotel room may be just as acceptable as a class A hotel room, but the hotel will not have facilities such as a conference room. Most hotels in class C and above are clean and reasonably furnished.

There are many lower-rated hotels, and relatively few in the higher categories. On the more popular islands such as Mykonos, Santorini, Skiathos or Kos, it is imperative to book in advance.

Most double rooms in Greece come with two single beds. If you wish to have a queen-size bed instead, be sure to specify a 'matrimonial' bed when you make your booking. Most hotels only have one or two rooms with queen-size beds.

If you travel in peak season, there may be a surcharge if you book for less than three days. Local and national taxes (around 4% and 8% respectively, plus a service charge of around 12%) will added to the posted price.

If you need advice, the Greek National Tourist Office (GNTO) can help with bookings and reservations. (Note that signs for GNTO offices in the islands read 'EOT'.) The GNTO (see TOURIST INFORMATION) has an information booklet on each island group that lists all hotels in the upper categories on the back page, complete with telephone numbers.

Private Accommodation Many families rent out rooms or studios to visitors. If you arrive without a reservation, consider this type of accommodation, particularly in peak season. If you arrive by ferry, there will be someone at the port with photographs to show you their accommodation. Private accommodation can be some distance from the main towns or resorts, so maintain a skeptical attitude towards any distances mentioned, and have a map ready so that the owner can point out exactly where the property is.

Villas For families or others who want to stay on one island for some time, renting a house or villa can be both cost-effective and a great way to see the island. Villas can be rented for a week or more, although some owners stipulate a one-month minimum. Always check exactly what facilities are provided. Most come with towels, bed linen and full kitchen facilities; some have pools and vehicles included in the rental. Tour operators and travel agents in your home country can assist you with bookings. Otherwise, contact the local office of the GNTO (see page 126).

AIRPORTS (see also GETTING THERE)

Most internationally scheduled flights land at the new Eleftherinos Venizolos International Airport <www.aia.gr>, which opened in 2002. The site of the old Athens Hellenikon International Airport is being developed as a public park and facilities for the 2004 Olympic Games. The airport acts as a hub for domestic flights to the islands. If you're heading into Athens, however, bear in mind that the new airport is some way out of the city in Spata. The most convenient way to get to the centre is on the E95 bus that runs to and from Syntagma Square (from where you can take the metro to elsewhere in the city).

If you want to travel direct from the airport to the port of Piraeus for onward ferry journeys, you can either go through the city or take another bus, the E96. Taxis from the airport are expensive, so the bus is probably the best option. If you do take a taxi, always insist that your driver turns on the meter at the start of your journey.

For the northern Aegean islands (Thasos, Limnos and Samothraki), it is possible to fly directly to Thessaloniki on the northern Greek mainland for ferry connections or onward flights.

The following islands have airports with a domestic service: Astypalea, Karpathos, Kastellorizo, Kos, Limnos, Milos, Mykonos, Lesvos

(Mytilini), Naxos, Paros, Samos, Santorini (Thira), Skiathos, Skyros and Syros. Many British and Irish package tour companies fly directly to some of the Greek islands. Kos, Skiathos, Lesvos and Mykonos are the main airports used.

ANTIQUITIES

The Greek authorities are very concerned about the loss of antiquities and other national treasures. If you intend to buy an old piece, be it an icon or a piece of statuary, always deal with a reputable dealer and keep your receipts. Genuine antiquities need a permit. Exporting antiquities without a permit is a serious offence.

B

BICYCLE AND MOTOR SCOOTER RENTAL

Bicycles Many islands and resorts are ideal places to rent bicycles, though some islands are too hilly to make it a viable way to tour around. But for those who want to cycle around the town or to the beach it is a useful form of transport. Bicycles can be rented in most major resorts for around €6 per day.

Motor Scooters Motor scooters or mopeds are very popular, and they can be one of the best ways to get around all but the largest Greek islands. Rental is relatively inexpensive (around €12 per day for a 50cc machine, lower if you hire one for three days or more). However, there are dangers in motorbike rental. Every year there are a number of serious injuries and fatalities involving motor cyclists. The government has recently passed legislation making it illegal to rent a machine with any size engine without a motorbike licence.

Many rental agencies have not passed on this information to hirers. If you rent a motorbike without a bike licence, any insurance you have will be null and void, creating grave difficulties for you if you are injured or involved in an accident. If you rent a bike or moped you should wear a helmet. Although it is rarely enforced, it is the law in

Greece. You should also proceed with caution, especially on corners where ground dust and gravel make the road surface slippery.

BUDGETING FOR YOUR TRIP

Once you have reached the Greek islands, living is relatively cheap. Food prices are controlled by the Greek government, and they rarely rise above the rate of inflation every year. Ferry travel and domestic flights are also affordable.

Here are some sample costs for goods and services in the islands:

Double room in moderately priced hotel	€50–75
One-day car rental	€50–80
One-day motor scooter rental	€12
Three-course dinner for one, without drinks	€15–20
One-way bus fare Parikia–Naoussa on Paros	€1
Taxi from Skiathos Airport to town	€3
Commercial ferry ticket, single fare, Mykonos–Paros	€5
Entrance fee to an archaeological site	€4
Half-hour Jet-ski rental	€12
Two-tank dive	€90

CAMPING

The climate of the Greek islands makes them a popular place for camping. The GNTO has a booklet with information about authorised camp sites, or you may wish to contact the Hellenic Camping Association, 102 Solonos Street, 106 80, Athens; Tel/fax 362 1560.

CAR HIRE (see also DRIVING)

Most islands have cars for hire, but think before you commit yourself. The primary roads on the major islands are usually in good condition, but if you want to explore secluded areas, the secondary roads may be of poor quality and require a 4-wheel drive vehicle.

On smaller or more popular islands, the local bus service may be adequate, with frequent services running from early morning until

11pm or later. Out of season, buses may not run at all during siesta (2pm–5pm) or after 6pm in the evening.

The following islands are large enough that car hire would enhance your stay and free you from complicated bus schedules: Tinos, Naxos, Paros, Skyros, Skopelos, Lesvos, Chios, Samos and Kos.

Booking through a major international firm before you arrive will guarantee your vehicle, which can be useful, especially in peak season. Hertz <www.hertz.co.uk>, Avis <www.avis.co.uk>, Europcar <www.europcar.co.uk> and Budget <www.budget.co.uk> all service the islands. However, there are many reputable local car hire agencies, including Reliable International (Syngrou 36–38, Athens, Tel. 210 924 9000). You may also find that local companies are more flexible with regards to price, especially in low season.

Most major car hire firms have offices at the island airport. If not, there may be an extra charge to deliver your car to the airport or to your hotel. Always ask if services such as delivery cost extra as the total fee for your rental may be disproportionately high with delivery included.

Those who wish to rent should carry an International Driving Permit, although a national driving licence is usually accepted (provided it has been held for one full year and the driver is over 21 years of age). Deposits are usually waived for those paying by credit card.
Insurance Insurance is often included in the hire charge, but enquire to be sure. The collision damage waiver is advisable. If your credit card or home insurance policy does not provide it, you should purchase it as part of your rental agreement.

C

CLIMATE

The Greek islands have a short, warm but rainy spring, a long, hot summer, a warm autumn and a cool winter. The northern islands are always a couple of degrees cooler than the southernmost. The islands are swept constantly by Meltemi winds, which blow from the Caucasus Mountains of Russia across the Black Sea and down into the Aegean. The Meltemi winds blow warm air in summer, but sometimes bitterly cold air in winter. The Cyclades are the most affected, where the winds can change daily.

Below is a chart of average monthly temperatures in °C and °F for Naxos in the central Cyclades.

		J	F	M	A	M	J	J	A	S	O	N	D
min	°C	10	9	11	13	16	20	22	22	21	18	14	12
	°F	50	49	51	56	61	68	72	72	69	64	58	53
max	°C	14	15	16	19	23	26	27	28	26	24	20	17
	°F	57	59	61	67	73	78	81	82	78	75	68	62

CLOTHING

In summer you'll require very little clothing in the Greek islands. In daytime, think about swimwear plus a light layer to protect you from sunburn, and sandals. For sightseeing, shorts or lightweight trousers and T-shirts are appropriate for men and women. Women will also be comfortable in lightweight dresses. Natural fibres such as cotton and silk are ideal, as they help to wick away perspiration and allow the skin to breathe. Be sure to pack comfortable walking shoes for touring archaeological sites.

If you intend to visit churches or monasteries, appropriate dress is compulsory. Both sexes should cover their shoulders. Men should wear lightweight trousers, not shorts, and women should wear a skirt that covers the knees. Don't forget a hat and good sunglasses. White-washed buildings reflect the sun, creating a lot of glare that can tire the eyes very quickly.

In the evening, the islands are relaxed. Very few places have a dress code, although visitors like to change for the evening. A light sweater would be useful for chilly evenings, especially in early or late season. Both spring and autumn can be cool after the sun has dropped.

It can also get remarkably chilly after dark on the decks of ferries, so if you take a day trip and intend to return late, a cotton sweater or fleece jacket might be welcome.

COMPLAINTS (see also EMERGENCIES)

If you have a complaint, it's best to raise it first with the proprietor of the establishment concerned. If you are not satisfied, then take your complaint to the tourist police (for telephone numbers, see EMERGENCIES). There is a contingent of officers on each island who deal solely with the security of visitors and process complaints of any kind. These officers speak English.

CRIME AND SAFETY (see also EMERGENCIES)

The Greek islands are relatively safe both in terms of your personal safety and the safety of your belongings. Most visitor problems tend to centre around motor scooter accidents and over-indulgence in sun or alcohol. Serious crime is rare; however, it is still important to guard against becoming a victim. Islands with the highest visitor numbers have reported an increase in theft and other petty crime, so make sure that you take the following precautions: lock any valuables in the hotel safe. Don't leave valuables unsupervised on the beach or in view in your hire car.

If you find yourself a victim of crime, contact the tourist police on the island concerned (for numbers on the main islands, see EMERGENCIES). These officers speak English.

CUSTOMS AND ENTRY REQUIREMENTS (see also ANTIQUITIES)

Citizens of Great Britain and Ireland, as EU citizens, can visit the Greek islands for an unlimited amount of time, but British citizens must have a valid passport. Citizens of Ireland can enter with a valid identity card or passport. Citizens of the US, Canada, Australia and New Zealand can stay for up to three months with a valid passport. South African citizens can stay for up to two months on a valid passport. No visas are needed for these stays. If you wish to extend these times, you must obtain a permit from the Aliens Bureau, 173 Alexandras Avenue, 11-522, Athens; Tel. 770 5701.

Visitors may import and export up to €10,000. There are no restrictions on traveller's cheques; however sums exceeding US$1,000 or its equivalent must be declared on entry.

Greece has some strict regulations regarding the import of drugs. All the obvious ones are illegal and there are punitive measures for anyone breaking the rules. Note that some seemingly benign drugs such as codeine or tranquillisers are also banned. If you take any drug on the advice of your doctor, always carry enough for your needs in an official container (medicines for personal use are permitted).

Since the abolishment of duty-free allowances for EU countries, all goods brought into Greece from Britain and Ireland must be duty paid. In theory, there are no limitations to the amount of duty-paid goods that can be brought into the country providing they are for personal use. The recommended limits are: 800 cigarettes, 200 cigars, 1 kg tobacco, 10 litres of spirits, 90 litres of wine. However, cigarettes and most spirits are much cheaper in Greece than in Britain and Ireland, therefore waiting until you reach your destination to buy these goods will save you money.

For citizens of non-EU countries, allowances for goods bought duty-free to be carried into Greece or the islands are as follows: 200 cigarettes or 50 cigars or 250 grams of tobacco; 1 litre of spirits or 4 litres of wine; 250 ml of cologne or 50 ml of perfume.

D

DRIVING

Road Conditions The roads in the Greek islands have improved in the last few years, although there are still great differences between A roads and B roads. The latter usually require a 4-wheel drive vehicle.

Most of the primary roads on the main islands have decent road surfaces, however the roads have no hard shoulders, only dust and stones at the side of the gravel. This can cause problems if you need to slow down and leave the carriageway, especially for motorcyclists who have to drive towards the centre of the paved surface to avoid the gravel. If you get caught in a summer storm, roads can become very slippery indeed.

Many roads are steep and narrow with switchback turns and no protection between the road and the drop – often precipitous – to the side. This requires a degree of concentration.

Rules and Regulations Greece drives on the right and passes on the left, usually yielding to vehicles from the right. Most road signs are international and easily understood, however one problem in navigating can be a lack of Roman transliterations of place names on road signs (just the Greek lettering appears).

The speed limit is 100 km/h (65 mph) on open roads; in towns, it is 50 km/h (30 mph), unless otherwise stated. Many drivers do not adhere to the regulations. Both speed limit and distance signs are in kilometres.

Seat belts are compulsory, as are crash helmets when riding a motor scooter. Drink-driving laws are strict. Road patrols are common, with Breathalyser tests and on-the-spot fines.

Many island towns have one-way streets. Be aware that motor scooter riders (and some car drivers) do not obey these rules. Motorcyclists may be both inexperienced and not properly insured, so give them a wide berth.

Pedestrians also have their own agendas. They will often walk in

Are we on the right road for…?	**Ímaste sto sostó drómo giá… ?**
Full tank, please.	**Na to gemísete me venzíni.**
Normal/super/lead-free.	**Aplí/soúper/amólivdos.**
My car has broken down.	**Epatha mía vlávi.**
There's been an accident.	**Egine éna disteíchima.**

the road and step out without looking. In towns, you may find a large number of backpackers who, carrying large and heavy packs in the heat, find it difficult to move out of the way. They appreciate a little latitude on the part of drivers.

Fuel Costs Petrol is extremely cheap by European standards at around €0.80 per litre. When exploring a large island, it's wise to anticipate your fuel needs, as petrol stations tend to be found only around the main towns. Petrol stations are open every day in season between the hours of 9am and 7pm.

Parking Car parks are marked by a sign with a white 'P' on a blue background. There is generally one public parking area in every major town, usually near the port. Most of the islands have painted lines along the roadside indicating whether parking is allowed. If you decide to park on the road, always check to make sure you are not creating a hazard for other drivers and users of the road. Do not park at intersections or near junctions, and do not block entrances. Most hotels and restaurants have car parking unless they are situated in old town centres, which tend to be pedestrian-only.

If You Need Help The Greek National Touring Club (ELPA), 2–4 Messogion Street, Athens; Tel. 779 1615, provides emergency road assistance (Tel. 104) in Greece, but in the islands this service is not comprehensive. Always take the local telephone number of your car-hire company when picking up your car or arranging for its delivery to you. If necessary, they can organise assistance for you.

Road Signs Most road signs are the standard pictographs used throughout Europe. However, you may also meet some of these written signs:

ΑΔΔΙΕΞΧΞΟΔΔΟΣΣ	No through road
ΑΛΛΑΤ/ΣΣΤΟΜ	Stop
ΑΝΩΩΩΜΑΑΛΛΑΙΑ ΟΔΔΔΟΣΣΤΡΩΩΩΜΑΤΟΣΣ	Bad road surface
ΑΠΡΠΑΓΓΓΟΡΕΥΕΤΑΙ Η ΕΙΣΣΣΟΔΔΔΟΣΣ	No entry

ΑΠΡΠΑΓΓΟΡΕΥΕΤΑΙ Η ΣΣΣΤΑΘΟΔΜΕΥΣΣΣΙΣΣ	No parking
ΔΔΔΙΑΒΑΣΣΣΙΣΣΣΠΡΠΕΖΩΩΩΝ	Pedestrian crossing
ΕΡΓΓΓΑ ΕΠΡΠΙ ΤΗΣΣΣ ΟΔΔΑΟΥ	Road works in progress
ΚΙΝΔΔΥΝΟΣΣΣ	Caution
ΜΟΝΟΔΓΡΟΜΟΣΣΣ	One-way traffic
ΠΡΠΑΡΑΚΑΜΠΡΠΤΗΡΙΟΣΣΣ	Diversion (detour)

E

ELECTRICITY

The electric current in Greece and the islands is 220 AC. Electric plugs are the standard round, two-pin European continental type. It's advisable to bring your own adapters. North American appliances will require transformers which are difficult to find in Greece.

EMBASSIES AND CONSULATES

Most countries have embassies and consulates in Athens, however some operate consular services on the islands.

Australia	37 D. Soutsou Street, 115-21, Athens; Tel. 645 0404; fax 646 6595
Canada	4 Gennadiou Street, 115-21, Athens; Tel. 727 3400; fax 727 3460
Ireland	7 Vass. Konstantinou Avenue, 106-74, Athens; Tel. 723 2771/2; fax 724 0217
New Zealand	24 Xanias Street, 115-28, Athens; Tel. 771 0112; fax 777 7390
South Africa	60 Kifissias Avenue, 151-25, Maroussi; Tel. 680 6645; fax 680 6640
United Kingdom	1 Ploutarchou Street, 106-75, Athens; Tel. 723 6211; fax 724 1872 or 723 0954
US	91 Vass. Sophias Avenue, 115-27, Athens; Tel. 721 2951; fax 645 6282

The UK also has the following regional consulates in the islands:

Kos   Tel. (02420) 21549; fax (02420) 25948
Syros   Tel. (02810) 82232; fax (02810) 83293

EMERGENCIES

Police presence on the islands is limited, and patrol cars are almost non-existent, although the chance of needing their help is also minimal. To reach the police, dial 100. There are tourist police officers on duty. These officers are specially trained to deal with visitor problems and speak English.

Here are the telephone numbers for the major islands:

Mykonos   Tel. 23990
Santorini   Tel. 22649
Kos   Tel. 22222
Skiathos   Tel. 21111

For medical emergencies, dial 166.

G

GAY AND LESBIAN TRAVELLERS

The island of Mykonos is one of the most gay-friendly destinations in Europe, with many beaches, hotels, bars and clubs specifically catering to gay and lesbian travellers (although gay and lesbian travellers are by no means limited to these places). July and August are the best months to meet like-minded people from all over Europe and participate in the most manic nightlife.

GETTING THERE (see also AIRPORTS, DRIVING)

By Air International scheduled flights will almost always land at Eleftherinos Venizolos International Airport <www.aia.gr>. For the northern Aegean Islands (Thasos, Limnos and Samothraki), it may be possible to fly direct to Thessaloniki on the northern Greek mainland for ferry connections or onward flights. The national airline for Greece and the Aegean islands is Olympic Airways (Tel. 0870 606 0460, <www.olympic-airways.co.uk>). It operates direct flights to and from the following destinations in the UK: London Gatwick and Heathrow airports (daily flights); Manchester and Glasgow airports (flights several times a week). In the US: New York (JFK) has daily flights, Boston has two a week. In Canada, there are flights to and from Montreal and Toronto twice a week. In Australia, Sydney has flights twice a week.

Other airlines that operate flights to Athens, which may provide connections for travellers from the US, South Africa, Ireland and Australasia include British Airways <www.ba.com> through London, KLM <www.klm.com> through Amsterdam and Lufthansa <www.lufthansa.co.uk> via Frankfurt.

Delta has direct flights to Athens from JFK Airport in New York.

Rather than buying a standard ticket, there are less expensive ways of flying to Athens and the islands. You may want to look at other options such as apex, stand-by and last-minute seats. Low-cost airlines with flights to Athens include EasyJet <www.easyjet.com>.

From Athens, Olympic Airways operates daily flights to the following Greek Islands: Chios, Kastellorizo (daily in summer only), Kos, Limnos, Milos, Mykonos, Lesvos (Mytilini), Naxos, Paros, Samos, Santorini (Thira), Skiathos and Syros, and operates several flights per week to Astypalea, Karpathos, and Skyros.

Olympic Airways will sometimes offer internal flights at a reduced rate for travellers who have flown into Greece on the airline. Ask about special deals before you make reservations. Unfortunately, it is almost impossible to travel from island to island by plane without returning to Athens, the hub of the system.

Charter flights from Britain also serve Kos, Skiathos, Lesvos and Mykonos during the summer months from London Gatwick, Manchester, and many regional airports. Ask your travel agent for details.

By Sea Travel to Athens and then take a ferry to your chosen island from the main harbours of Piraeus or Rafina on the Greek mainland.

From Eleftherinos Venizolos International Airport take a bus or taxi to the port of Piraeus for onward ferry journeys to the islands (see AIRPORTS for details).

Cruising is a popular option, and a comfortable way to see several islands in a short space of time. A number of companies offer the Aegean Islands as an itinerary (Mykonos/Delos and Santorini are favourites), with starting ports at either Istanbul or Athens. Ships offer different levels of service, and thus price ranges, so research is imperative in order to get the package that suits your taste and budget. Cunard <www.cunardline.com> is one of the long-standing companies. Royal Olympic Cruise Line <www.royalolympiccruises.com> is a company based in Greece.

By Car The direct road route to Greece and the islands from Western Europe takes travellers through the former Yugoslavia, which for obvious reasons has been less popular in recent years. However, for those who want to travel from Western Europe with a vehicle, there are several ferry companies that operate services from ports in Italy to ports on the Greek mainland.

Patras to Bari (17 hours) and Patras to Ancona (20 hours) are the main routes. Two operators are Superfast Ferries, 157 Alkyonidon Avenue, 166-73, Voula, Athens; Tel. (210) 969 1100, fax (210) 969 1190, <www.superfast.com>; and Strintzis Lines, 26 Akti Possidonis, 185-31, Piraeus; Tel. (210) 414 1230; fax (210) 422 5256, <www.strintzis.gr>.

In order to enter Greece, you must have the vehicle registration document, a nationality plate, and proof of insurance (a comprehensive plan is advised).

By Rail Travelling through Europe to Greece by train poses the same problems as car travel, because all major rail services cross through the states of the former Yugoslavia. Rail travel can still be accomplished by taking services to the Italian ferry ports and taking a boat as by the 'By Car' section above. Eurorail <www.eurorail.com> has several combination tickets, including special fares for those who are under the age of 26 and senior citizens.

GUIDES AND TOURS

If you wish to engage the services of an English-speaking guide, contact the GNTO (EOT in the islands) to discuss possibilities on each island (see TOURIST INFORMATION). Taxi drivers will undertake half-day tours for an agreed fee, but will not act as guides.

Each island has travel agencies that can arrange itineraries and activities. Below are ones that we have found particularly helpful: Nirvana Tours on the seafront at Petra on Lesvos, Tel. (02530) 41991, fax (02530) 41992; Theokritos Travel on the main street in Tigaki on Kos; Tel. (02420) 69666, fax (02420) 69112.

H

HEALTH AND MEDICAL CARE (see also CUSTOMS AND ENTRY REQUIREMENTS)

In a medical emergency, dial 166. Each island has a hospital with doctors who speak reasonable English.

Emergency treatment is given free of charge to visitors, but this covers only immediate treatment. EU residents (UK and Irish nationals) will be able to get further free treatment, but must carry the form E111 to obtain it. E111 forms must be validated before you leave the UK. This is done at the post office before you depart for your trip.

It is always advisable to take out health/accident insurance to cover you for a health emergency while on holiday. Check that the insurance will reimburse the cost of protracted treatment, an air taxi from smaller islands to the nearest major hospital, or repatriation should the need arise.

There are no vaccination requirements for the Greek islands.

The Greek islands do have scorpions and snakes, although not in great numbers, and they tend only to be found off the beaten track. When exploring archaeological sites, it is always wise to watch your footing and make some noise to ensure that the creatures have time to escape before you arrive. A more common nuisance is the mosquito, especially on a balmy night. Always carry and use anti-mosquito spray when walking in the undergrowth and when the sun sets.

Spiny sea urchins cause a number of injuries each year when people step on them while swimming. Avoidance is the best option, so invest in plastic sandals to protect your feet.

The sun is strong in Greece, especially as the summer breezes seem to cool the air, so it is important to use appropriate protection. Limit your time in the sun, apply sunblock regularly and always carry a cover-up with you in case of overexposure. Children's skin should be well-protected when they are out in the sunshine.

Go easy on alcohol, it can cause dehydration. Tap water is safe to drink; however, bottled water often tastes better and is universally available. Always carry water with you to the beach or when sightseeing to protect against dehydration.

Pharmacies A pharmacy (*pharmakio*) is marked by a sign with a green cross. Most pharmacists speak some English and will dispense medical advice for minor ailments such as sunburn.

HOLIDAYS

During national holidays, government offices close along with most museums and archaeological sites. Restaurants and shops may remain open, especially during the tourist season. National holidays fall on the following dates:

1 January	New Year's Day (*Protochroniá*)
6 January	Epiphany (*Ton*)
25 March	Greek Independence Day
1 May	May Day
15 August	Assumption of the Virgin
28 October	'No' Day (*Ochi*)
25 December	Christmas Day
26 December	St Stephen's Day

Movable dates occur around Easter. The first day of Lent (Clean Monday), Good Friday, Easter Monday, Ascension Day and Holy

Monday (otherwise known as Whit Monday) change with every calendar year.

L

LANGUAGE

The Greek language of Homer and the ancients is no longer spoken in daily life. There are two Greek languages: *katharévousa*, which is the language of the elite, the courts and of the ancient texts; and *dimotikí*, which is the language written and spoken by most Greek people today.

The majority of people working in the tourist industry have a basic English vocabulary and many speak English very well.

The table below lists the Greek letters in their capital and small forms, followed by the letters to which they correspond in English.

A	α	a	α	a as in **bar**
B	β	b	β	v
G	Γ	g	γ	g as in **go***
D	Δ	d	δ	d like **th** in **this**
E	ε	e	ε	e as in **get**
Z	ζ	z	ζ	z
H	ή	h	ή	i like **ee** in **meet**
Q	Θ	q	θ	th as in **thin**
I	ι	i	ι	like **ee** in **meet**
K	κ	k	κ	k
L	Λ	l	λ	l
M	μ	m	μ	m
N	ν	n	ν	n
X	Ξ	x	ξ	x like **ks** in **thanks**
O	o	o	o	as in **got**
P	Π	p	π	p
P	ρ	r	ρ	r
S	Σ	s	σ, ς	s as in **kiss**

T	τ	t	τ	t
Y	υ	u	υ	i like **ee** in m**ee**t
F	Φ	j	φ	f
X	χ	c	χ	ch as in Scottish lo**ch**
Y	Ψ	y	ψ	ps as in ti**ps**y
O	O/Ω	w	ω	o as in g**o**t
OY	ου	ou	ου	oo as in s**ou**p

*except before i- and e-sounds, when it's pronounced like y in yes.
You'll find the *Berlitz Greek Phrase Book and Dictionary* covers
nearly all the situations you're likely to encounter in your travels.

M

MAPS

Toubis prints maps that cover all of the Aegean Islands. The maps are
simple but feature the main tourist sites and the road network
(M. Toubis S.A.; Tel. 9923874, <www.toubis.gr>). They are available
at most bookshops and newsagents.

MEDIA

The only English-language newspaper that offers an insight into
Greek and world affairs is *Athens Today*, which can be bought at
most newsagents. There is at least one newsagent on each of the
main islands, either near the port or in the town square. Major
English-language newspapers can be bought on the most-visited
islands, although they will be at least one day old. All UK dailies
can be purchased, along with the *New York Times*.

If it is important to be totally up-to-date, then try getting online at
one of the internet cafés that are springing up on islands such as Paros,
Naxos, Mykonos and Santorini.

Only a small number of hotels have satellite television. A few may
offer an English-language TV news service – generally BBC News
24 – along with services in other languages.

MONEY

Currency Greece's monetary unit is the euro (abbreviated €), which is divided into 100 cents. Banknotes are available in denominations of 500, 200, 100, 50, 20, 10 and 5 euros. There are coins for 2 and 1 euros, and for 50, 20, 10, 5, 2 and 1 cents.

Currency Exchange Most banks offer currency exchange for foreign currencies and travellers' cheques, charging a commission for the service that varies, but is usually between 1% and 3%. Exchange rates should be published on a notice board inside the bank or in the window, and are generally the same for each bank.

You can also exchange money and traveller's cheques at bureaux de change found in the tourist centres of the main islands. The bureaux are often open longer hours than banks. Some of them advertise commission-free transactions, but exchange rates vary, so you'll need to judge which establishment offers the better deal.

You will always need to prove your identity when exchanging money, so take your passport with you.

Traveller's Cheques These are best exchanged for cash at banks or bureaux de change rather than being used to buy goods directly.

Automatic Teller Machines (ATMs) Using an ATM is the most convenient way of obtaining euros, and depending on your own individual card charges, it might also be the cheapest. There is a good network of ATMs throughout the major islands that will accept both major credit cards (MasterCard and Visa) and debit cards (Cirrus and Plus). However, long queues can develop at busy times of year, and machines can be either empty or out of order, so it would not be sensible to rely on ATMs as your sole means of obtaining cash.

Credit Cards Many hotels, restaurants, ticket offices and shops accept credit cards, but there is still a sizeable minority which do not. Some may charge extra for credit card payments, to cover their costs. It is always advisable to ask about credit card acceptance before you sign the register or order your food, to avoid difficulties later. It may also help to carry cash – perhaps £15–£25 ($25–$35) per person per day – to cover meals, rather than rely on your credit card. On the more remote islands, cash is always the safest bet for everyday transactions.

O

OPENING HOURS

Opening hours can be a little complicated. They vary greatly between high and low season on the most popular islands. Always be aware that the siesta is an important part of the day, and most establishments will close in the afternoon.

Banks are open Mon–Thurs 8am–2pm, Fri 8am–1.30pm.

Most museums are open Mon–Fri 8am–2pm and 5pm–7pm (this will vary). Most archaeological sites are closed on Monday.

Shops are open Mon–Sat 8am–2pm and 5pm–8.30pm, although in peak season, they may stay open until midnight. Post offices open Mon–Sat 8am–2pm; on the larger islands, they may remain open until 7pm.

P

POLICE (see also EMERGENCIES)

To reach the police, dial 100. To reach the tourist police on a particular island, consult the list below:

Kos   Tel. (02420) 22222
Mykonos   Tel. (02890) 23990
Santorini Tel. (02860) 22649
Patmos   Tel. (02470) 31303
Skiathos   Tel. (04270) 21111

POST OFFICES

Post office signs are painted bright yellow with the initials ELTA. They are generally open from 8am–2pm. Stamps can be bought here at cost and from newsagents for a small premium. Parcels for non-EU countries should not be sealed until they have been checked by post office staff. Post offices also handle currency exchange, and cash cheques and money orders. Postage for a postcard to the UK is around €0.70, and it generally takes five to seven days to arrive.

PUBLIC TRANSPORT

Most islands have a good bus service that connects all major settlements and beaches. A small central bus station posts a timetable for each route, with a regular, generally on-time service. Buses may stop during the afternoon siesta, although this is generally the case only on small islands.

How much is it to go to…?	**Piá íne i timí giá… ?**
bus stop	**stásis**
single	**apló**
return	**me epistrofí**

Fares are low. In addition, a small boat (caique) service often runs from major resorts to popular beaches. These boats are usually cheap and reliable.

R

RELIGION

The Greek Orthodox religion is most prevalent throughout the islands. There are also Catholic churches on a few islands, notably on Tinos and Naxos.

T

TELEPHONE

The country code for Greece is 30. To call overseas from the Greek islands, dial 00, then the country code, then the telephone number. For reference, Australia is 61, Canada is 1, Ireland is 353, New Zealand is 64, South Africa is 27, the UK is 44 and the US is 1.

There are many card-operated telephone booths throughout the islands, usually at ports. Directions appear in English on most machines. Newsagents and hotels sell telephone cards which can be used for domestic and direct-dial international calls.

TIME ZONES

Greece is two hours ahead of Greenwich mean time (GMT). The chart below compares Greek time with other time zones worldwide.

	New York	London	**Aegean**	Jo'burg	Sydney
winter:	5am	10am	**12noon**	12noon	9pm
summer:	5am	10am	**12noon**	11am	7pm

TIPPING

Service is included in restaurant and bar bills, although it is customary to leave any small change on the table.

Taxi drivers expect a 10% tip. Hotel chambermaids should be left a tip of around €1 per day. Doormen and porters should be tipped up to €2 depending on services provided. Attendants in toilets should be left around €0.30.

TOILETS

You will generally find public toilets near the market squares in most main towns on the islands; look for the international signs of a figure of a man or a woman. They are of varying degrees of cleanliness and will often be of a 'hole-in-the-floor' design rather than a sit-down variety. Most cafés and bars have clean facilities, although these may be basic. It is customary to buy a drink at an establishment if you wish to use the toilets. On beaches, the bars and cafés have toilets. Remember, never put toilet tissue into the toilet; Greek drains become clogged very easily. Always use the receptacle provided. If there is an attendant present, it is customary to leave a small tip.

TOURIST INFORMATION

The Greek National Tourist Organisation (GNTO) or Ellinikos Organismos Tourismu (EOT) is responsible for producing and disseminating tourist information. They have a network of offices throughout the world, but official representation in the islands is very scant. This leaves the market open to lots of unofficial information bureaux, which vary greatly in quality. For tourist information before you travel to Greece, contact one of the following offices:

Australia and New Zealand	51-75 Pitt Street, Sydney, New South Wales (PO Box R203, Royal Exchange, New South Wales 2000); Tel. (2) 92411663-5; fax 92352174
Canada	1300 Bay Street, Main Level, Toronto, Ontario M5R 3K8; Tel. (416) 968-2220; fax (416) 968 6533; e-mail <gnto.tor@sympatico.ca>
UK and Ireland	4 Conduit Street, London W1R 0DJ; Tel. (020) 7734 5997; fax (020) 7287 1369; e-mail <info@gnto.co.uk>
US	Olympic Tower, 645 Fifth Avenue, New York, NY 10022; Tel. (212) 421-5777; fax (212) 826 6940; e-mail <info@greektourism.com>

For tourist information in the Aegean, official GNTO/EOT offices can be found at the following addresses:

Athens	2 Amerikis Street, PO Box 1017, 105-64 Athens; Tel. (210) 327-1300; fax (210) 322 4184
Cyclades Islands	10 Dodecanissou Street, 841-00, Syros; Tel. (08210) 86725; fax (08210) 82375
Limnos	Provincial Buildings of Limnos, 814-00, Limnos; Tel. (02540) 22996
Northeast Aegean	6 T. Aristarchou Street, 811-00, Mytilini (Lesvos), Tel. (02510) 42511; Airport at Mytilini (Lesvos), Tel. (02510) 61279
Samos	4 25th March Street, 831-00, Samos; Tel. (02730) 28530

W

WEBSITES

There are a number of websites to help you to plan your trip. Although information and sites are changing constantly, here are some that should prove useful.

The official GNTO sites:

<www.gnto.co.uk>

<www.gnto.gr>

<www.greektourism.com>.

Other sites of interest include:

<www.greecetravel.com>

<www.greekhotels.com>

<www.helios.gr>

<www.hri.org>

<www.gtpnet.com>

WEIGHTS AND MEASURES

The metric system is used in Greece.

Y

YOUTH HOSTELS

The Greek Youth Hostel Association (4 Dragatsaniou Street, 105-59, Athens, Tel. 323-4107) can provide information about youth hostels in the islands. We can recommend two youth hostels in Santorini (Kamares Youth Hostel, Erythrou Stavrou, Tel. (02860) 22387; and Kondohori Youth Hostel, Agios Eleftherios, Tel. (02860) 22722), but the many cheap private rooms around the islands make the need for hostels less pressing than elsewhere.

Recommended Hotels

Although there is a great deal of accommodation scattered throughout the Aegean Islands, the majority of it is in the lower quality range, with many C-rated hotels and unclassified small studio apartments. If you intend to travel in the summer months and want a good-quality hotel, always make a firm reservation before you travel. If you arrive without a booking, there are a number of private agencies that advertise booking services. You will generally find them at the port.

Prices vary greatly during the season with the highest rates from early July to the end of August. In early season (Easter–mid-June) and late season (after mid-September), discounts are possible.

Most hotels will make a reservation for room only or bed and breakfast. In some cases, you can book full board (American plan), but for most people, eating out is one of the most enjoyable aspects of an Aegean Island holiday.

As a guide to room prices, we have used the following euro symbols for double occupancy with bath, including breakfast, mid-season:

€€€€€	over 80 euros
€€€€	65–80 euros
€€€	50–65 euros
€€	35–50 euros
€	under 35 euros

THE CYCLADES

MYKONOS

Belvedere Hotel €€€€€ *Rochari, 84600, Mykonos; Tel. 22890-25122/5; fax (22890) 25126; web site: www.belvederehotel.com* Set just outside the hustle and bustle of the centre of town, the Belvedere is housed in a white Cyclades-style building with an excellent pool. Internet facilities are provided, and Jacuzzi and steam baths are available. Guest laundry facilities. Buffet-style breakfast served daily 7–10.30am. Open all year-round. 40 rooms. Major credit cards.

Leto Hotel €€€€ *Hora, 84600, Mykonos; Tel. (22890) 22207; fax (22890) 23985; e-mail <leto@leto.myk.forthnet.gr>*. An easy five-minute walk from the port, this property is ideally located. It's near the town museum (approximately 10 minutes by foot from the town centre) with excellent views looking across a small fishing harbour. Set in lush gardens with an attractive secluded pool. Buffet-style breakfast served daily 7–10.30am. Open year-round. 25 rooms. Major credit cards.

Tharroe of Mykonos €€€€€ *Hora, 84600, Mykonos; Tel. (22890) 27370/4; fax (22890) 27375*. Located just outside the town, this luxury resort is housed in a typical Cyclades-style white-washed building. All rooms are equipped with mini-bars, safes and telephones. Facilities include 24-hour room service, a fitness room, sauna, pool and terrace. Free transfers are available. Buffet-style breakfast served daily 7–10.30am. Open year-round. 25 rooms. Major credit cards.

Theoxenia Hotel €€€ *Hora, 84600, Mykonos; Tel. (22890) 22230/23008; fax (22890) 22240; e-mail <theoxenia@leto.myk.forthnet.gr>*. Situated on the beach a little way south of Mykonos Town and near the windmills, the Theoxenia is housed in a traditional whitewashed building. Most rooms have a sea view. Buffet-style breakfast served daily 7–10.30am. Open April–October. 57 rooms. Major credit cards.

TINOS

Hotel Tinion €€ *1 Constantinou Alavanou, 84200, Tinos; Tel. (22830) 22261/24754; fax (22830) 24754*. A traditional, family-run hotel with simply furnished rooms. Located one street back from the harbour of Tinos Town. Some of the rooms are equipped with air-conditioning and have balconies overlooking the street and harbour. Breakfast served daily 7–10am. Open April–October. 20 rooms. Major credit cards.

PAROS

Astir of Paros €€€€€ *Kolymbithres, Naoussa, 84401, Paros; Tel. (22840) 51976; fax (22840) 51985; e-mail <astir @prometheus.hol.gr>.* An opulent resort hotel with a private beach, beautiful gardens, tennis courts, Jacuzzi, gym and 3-hole golf course. All rooms have air-conditioning, telephones, mini-bars, TVs and room service. Open April–November. 46 rooms. Major credit cards.

Dina € *Parikia, 84400, Paros; Tel. (22840) 23525.* Small, friendly hotel located in the heart of the old town. Spotlessly clean rooms set around a lovely courtyard with lots of flowers. Open April–October. Only eight rooms, so it is advisable to book early.

Lefkes Village Hotel €€€€€ *Lefkes, 84400, Paros; Tel. (22840) 41827; fax (22840) 41827. Winter: 137 Irakliou Avenue, 111 42, Athens; Tel. (210) 251 6497; fax (210) 253 3598.* This Cycladic-style hotel situated just outside Lefkes village has beautifully styled rooms and communal areas, a pool and a terrace with majestic panoramic views down a verdant valley. The complex has a large garden, winery and folklore museum. All rooms have air-conditioning, telephones and mini-bars. Open April–end of October. 20 rooms of two, three and four beds. Major credit cards.

NAXOS

Hotel Grotta €€–€€€ *Hora (Naxos Town), 84300, Naxos; Tel. (22850) 22215; fax (22850) 22000; e-mail <grotta@naxos-is-land.com>.* A friendly, family-run hotel that's ideally situated on a hillside in the heart of the old town, within easy walking distance of the ferry port. Open April–October. 40 rooms. Cash only.

Mathiassos Village €€–€€€ *Hora, 84300, Naxos; Tel. (22850) 23300; winter Tel. (210) 291 8749 or (22850) 22318.* Bungalows built in the Cycladic style surrounded by large and verdant gardens on the outskirts of Hora. Facilities include a restaurant/café, swimming pool, children's playground, tennis court and bus service to the beach (a 10-minute walk away). Open March–October. 110 rooms. Major credit cards.

SANTORINI

Esperides € *Kamari, 84700, Santorini; Tel. (22860) 31185.* Small, friendly new hotel, situated in a pistachio grove which includes the ruins of a Byzantine town. The volcanic, black sand beach is just 50 m (164 ft) away. The rooms are equipped with a refrigerator and telephone and have a balcony overlooking either the sea or the village. Air-conditioning is available. Open April–October. 39 rooms.

Fanari Traditional Cave Apartments €€€€€ *Oia, 84702, Santorini; Tel. (22860) 71008; fax (22860) 71235.* These refurbished, traditional cave houses have spectacular views. They spill down the caldera edge at the northern tip of Ia settlement, a five-minute walk from the town centre. The pool is cut into a hillside, with half of it in the sunlight. Open April–October. 12 units. Major credit cards.

Hotel Veggara €€€€ *On the seafront, Perissa, 84700, Santorini; Tel. (22860) 82060; fax (22860) 82608. Athens office: 72 Archelaou Street, 13671, Thrakomakedones, Athens; Tel. (210) 243 1411; fax (210) 243 0168.* Housed in a neo-classical main building with surrounding Cycladic-style studios, the Veggara has pretty, well-appointed rooms. Two pools with a bar sit just off the beach. Studios and apartments have fully fitted kitchens. All rooms, studios and apartments have air-conditioning, TVs, telephones and patios or balconies. Open May–November. 23 rooms, 9 studios and 8 apartments. Major credit cards.

Santorini Palace €€€€€ *Fira, 84700, Santorini; Tel. (22860) 22771; fax (22680) 23705; e-mail <spalace@otenet.gr>.* Located about a 10-minute walk from the centre of Fira, the Santorini Palace sits 100 m (300 ft) from the caldera edge, with views over the coastal plains. The hotel has a pool with bar, a restaurant and room service. Rooms have air-conditioning, telephones, satellite TVs, mini-bars and hairdryers. Open year-round. 106 rooms. Major credit cards.

THE DODECANESE

KOS

Neptune Hotel €€€€ *Mastichari, 85300, Kos; Tel. (22420) 41480; fax (22420) 41574.* Perhaps the largest resort in the Aegean. Set among 170 acres in three separate developments, the Neptune is 30 minutes by car from Kos Town. Facilities include a sauna and Jacuzzi, tennis courts, three pools, three children's pools, a hairdresser and a social programme. All rooms have TVs, mini-bars, kitchenettes, safes and hair dryers. Open April–November. 485 rooms. Major credit cards.

Paradise Hotel €–€€ *22 Odos Bouboulinas, Kos Town; Tel. (22420) 22988; fax (22420) 24205.* Located in the heart of Kos Town, this hotel is well situated for exploring nearby archaeological sites, taking the ferry, or enjoying the nightlife. Basic rooms but extremely friendly service. Open May–October. 100 rooms. Major credit cards.

KARPATHOS

Panorama € *Vrondi, behind the start of the beach; Tel. (22450) 23262; fax (22450) 23021.* Reasonably sized rooms equipped with refrigerators, overlooking either the sea or orchard.

PATMOS

Blue Bay Hotel €€€ *Skala, 85500, Patmos; Tel. (22470) 31165; fax (02470) 32303.* Situated a two-minute walk south of the town of Skala, the Blue Bay looks out over the entrance to the harbour. A small hotel, it has a no-smoking policy. Rooms are large and bright. There is also a bar and Internet café. Open April–October. 27 rooms. Cash only.

The Kastelli Hotel €€ *Skala, 85500, Patmos; Tel. (22470) 31361; fax (02470) 31656.* Set back from the seafront, this hotel stands behind the Skala Hotel. The rooms are clean and bright with balconies overlooking the harbour. Wonderful morning sunshine for early risers. Open year-round. 45 rooms. Cash only.

Skala Hotel €€€€ *Skala, 85500, Patmos; Tel. (22470) 31343; fax (22470) 31347; winter Tel. (210) 453 4000; fax (210) 453 0550; e-mail <skalahtl@12net.gr>.* Situated on the harbourfront, the Skala is ideally located for exploring the village. It's close to the ferry, tavernas and shopping. The hotel has a small pool and terrace, a bar and restaurant. All rooms have mini-bars. Open 1 April–31 October. 70 rooms. Major credit cards.

THE EASTERN AEGEAN

LESVOS

The Delfinia €€€ *Molyvos, 81108, Lesvos; Tel. (22530) 71373; fax (22530) 71524.* On the seafront at Molyvos, this hotel features rooms and bungalows. There is a good-size pool and beautiful views of the town. Rooms have telephones and balconies; bungalows have air-conditioning and mini-bars. Open year-round. 125 rooms. Major credit cards.

The Olive Press Hotel €€€€ *Molyvos, 81108, Lesvos; Tel. (22530) 71205; fax (22530) 71647.* This hotel was once an olive press and lies on the seafront where boats used to take the barrels of oil away. A relaxing ambience pervades the whole establishment. Open April–October. 50 rooms. Major credit cards.

Hotel Sea Horse €€ *The Harbour, Molyvos, 81108, Lesvos; Tel. (22530) 71630; fax (22530) 71374.* Basic rooms with refrigerators, but all overlook the picturesque harbour. Open from Greek Easter to the end of October. 17 rooms. Cash only.

Hotel Votsala €€ *Thermi, GR, 81100, Lesvos; Tel. (22510) 71231; fax (22510) 71179. Winter: 17 Kydonion, Smyrni, GR, 17121, Athens; Tel/fax (210) 933 8887.* Set in a little spa village on the east coast of Lesvos, this small seashore hotel operates in a relaxed, house-party style. The owner leads archaeological walks for guests every week in summer. Restaurant and bar. All rooms have refrigerators and balconies. Open April–October. 42 rooms. Major credit cards.

CHIOS

Hotel Chios Chandris €€€ *Prokimea, Chios Town; Tel. (22710) 44401; fax (22710) 25768.* By Greek island standards, this is a high-rise hotel that dominates the harbourfront. Rooms were updated in the late 1990s and have air-conditioning, mini-bars and TVs. Roof garden restaurant, large pool. Open year-round. 156 rooms. Major credit cards.

Volissos Traditional Houses €€–€€€€ *Volissos Village, Chios; Tel. (22740) 21421; fax (22740) 21521.* Accommodation is in restored stone houses in a typical Greek village. All are tastefully and sympathetically decorated and sit among real family homes. Open April–October. 15 units of one or two bedrooms. Cash only.

SAMOS

Doryssa Bay Hotel and Village €€€€ *Pythagorio, 83100, Samos; Tel. (22730) 61360; fax (22730) 61463.* A large, modern resort complex with a swimming pool, tennis courts, water sports facilities and children's playground. Open April–October. 302 rooms. Major credit cards.

Galini €€ *Pythagorio, 83100, Samos; Tel. (22730) 61167.* Modern, small, quiet self-catering rooms near the top of the town. Unusually for Samos, the Galini welcomes guests without a reservation. Open April–October. 9 rooms.

The Samos Hotel €€€–€€€€ *11 Themofolis Sofouli Street, 83100, Samos; Tel. (22730) 28377; fax (22730) 28482.* The Samos is on the promenade at Samos Town, near the ferry – a great location for touring the island. Facilities include swimming pool, Jacuzzi and 24-hour room service. Rooms contain TV and phone and have a balcony. Open all year. 50 rooms. Major credit cards.

Vathy € *Ano Vathy, 83100, Samos; Tel. (22730) 28124; fax (22730) 24045.* The relative distance of this hotel, situated in the old part of Vathy, is compensated for by the warmth of the reception. The rooms have a mini-bar and views of the bay. Small pool. Open April–October. 11 rooms.

THE SPORADES

SKIATHOS

Hotel Alkyon €€€ *Amoundia, Skiathos Town; Tel. (24270) 22981; fax (24270) 21643.* On the seafront just outside Skiathos Town, the Alkyon is close to restaurants and nightlife; the ferry is only a five-minute walk away. There is also a small pool. Open April–October. 88 rooms. Major credit cards.

Atrium Hotel €€€€ *37002, Skiathos; Tel. (24270) 49345; fax (24270) 49444.* Situated on a headland above pretty beaches, the Atrium is about 15 minutes by bus from Skiathos Town. A beautifully styled hotel – the communal areas were based on traditional monastery buildings. Fitness room and large pool with a terrace and bar. All rooms have patios or balconies plus air-conditioning and telephones. Open April–November. 75 rooms. Major credit cards.

Skiathos Palace €€€€€ *Koukounaries Beach, 37002, Skiathos; Tel. (24270) 22242; fax (24270) 49666.* A luxury resort set on the hillside above Koukounaries Beach. Facilities include a nightclub, swimming pool, sauna, water sports centre and tennis courts. Room service. Open May–October. 223 rooms. Major credit cards.

SKOPELOS

Skopelos Village €€€–€€€€ *Skopelos Town, 37003, Skopelos; Tel. (24240) 22517; fax (24240) 22958.* Ten minutes from Skopelos Town, this complex has a swimming pool, children's playground and room service. Each apartment has a small kitchen and up to two bedrooms. Bus transfer to nearby beaches. Open April–October. 36 apartments. Major credit cards.

Recommended Restaurants

The following recommendations are scattered across the main Greek islands and range from authentic *ouzeries* and good-value tavernas to some of the most renowned restaurants in the region. Some are a little hard to find, having no address in the accepted sense. If this is the case, ask at your hotel for directions. A little effort to find authentic cuisine always pays dividends, so be on the lookout for small back-street establishments that are sure to be frequented by local people.

Most restaurants do not operate a booking system. Where reservations are recommended, we have indicated it in the description.

The price categories used in this section are based on the cost of a main course for one person. Prices for appetisers are very similar wherever you eat in the Aegean (Greek salads are around €3 and *mezedes* range from €2.50 to €5)

€€€€€	over 18 euros
€€€€	12–18 euros
€€€	8–12 euros
€€	4–8 euros
€	under 4 euros

THE CYCLADES

MYKONOS

Edem €€€–€€€€ *near Panagia Panahrandou (the church at the top of the hill); Tel. (22890) 22855/23355.* Open year-round, daily 12 noon–1am. Upmarket restaurant set around a swimming pool. Very atmospheric in the evening, or you can have a swim before lunch. Greek dishes with a continental twist. Reservations recommended in peak season. Major credit cards.

Remvi €€€–€€€€ *at the Belvedere Hotel; Tel. (22890) 25122.* Open April–October, daily 8am–midnight. A relaxing and upmarket eatery with outstanding views over Mykonos Town from its terrace. Serves *à la carte* menu of Greek and Continental dishes that changes regularly. Reservations recommended. Major credit cards.

Taverna Antonini €€ *Platia Manto (where the taxi rank is); Tel. (22890) 22319.* Busy taverna spilling out onto a side street off the Platia Manto. Good Greek fare and friendly service. It's been in business since the 1950s. Cash only.

Taverna Vaggelis €€ *Platia Anomeras (the square in Ano Mera); Tel. (22890) 71577.* Open April–end of October, daily 11am–midnight. Typical Greek taverna with fresh fish and an open barbecue. Excellent dishes (staples of Greek cuisine) and a friendly atmosphere – a favourite with Greek families. Cash only.

PAROS

Apollon €€€ *Market Street, 88400, Paros; Tel. (22840) 21875.* Open April–October, daily 5pm-midnight. Set in the buildings and walled gardens of an old olive press, the Apollon offers a relaxing ambience and wonderfully cooked authentic Greek dishes. The food and service are worth the higher prices charged here. Major credit cards.

Babis Sarris € *Market Street, Parikia; Tel. (22840) 22702.* Open April–October, daily 9am-1am; November–May, Friday, Saturday and Sunday only 9am–1am. Don't be put off by the modern décor of this *psistaria* (barbecue-style restaurant), the salad ingredients and meat come from the family farm and add an extra delicious touch to the *gyros* (thin slices of meat cut from a spit and served on pitta bread), *souvlakis* (small chunks of meat served on a skewer) and Greek salads. Cash only.

Barbarossa €–€€€ *on the harbour at Naoussa, No phone.* Open year-round, daily 11am–11pm. This is only one of several authentic *ouzeries* along the harbour – all are good. Delicious *mezedes* are a speciality, especially octopus dishes. Sit with the elderly fishermen and watch the world go by. Cash only.

NAXOS

Kastro €€ *Plateia Prandounas, Naxos Town; Tel. (22850) 22005.* Open year-round, daily 7pm–2am. Set in a small square with fine views over the harbour, the Kastro overflows with tables in summer and specialises in dishes made with locally caught rabbit. Try the rabbit stew with onions and red wine sauce. Cash only.

SANTORINI

Restaurant 1800 €€€€ *Odos Nikolaos Nomikos, Ia; Tel. (22860) 71485.* Open April–October daily for lunch 12 noon–4pm and dinner 7.30pm–1am. Set in a refurbished mansion (named after the date when it was originally built) which once belonged to a sea captain, this is one of the prettiest places on the island to eat or have a drink at the bar. Greek and Continental dishes. Major credit cards.

Selene €€€–€€€€ *near the Artessena Hotel, Fira, Santorini; Tel. (22860) 23427.* Open year-round daily for lunch 12 noon–3pm and dinner 7pm–midnight. A superb setting on the caldera and fine cuisine with attention to detail has made Selene one of the top restaurants in the Aegean. Greek dishes with an international accent. Reservations recommended. Major credit cards.

Taverna Nikolas €–€€€ *off the main square, Fira; Tel. (22860) 24550.* Open March–October, daily 12 noon–midnight. This small, family-run taverna is the place to meet local people. The food is freshly cooked daily, so there is no set menu. The dining room is always lively and very busy – expect to queue. Cash only.

Vanilia €€€ *84700 Firostefani Square, Firostefani; Tel. (22860) 25931.* Open April–September daily for lunch 12 noon–4pm and dinner 5.30pm–1am. Situated on the crater, a 10-minute walk north of the centre of Fira, this intimate restaurant offers a relaxing ambience. Whitewashed stone benches are covered with comfortable ethnic cushions and low lighting sets the scene. Several small rooms mean a quiet intimate dining experience. Greek and European dishes. Major credit cards.

THE DODECANESE

KOS

Petrino €€€–€€€€ *Plateia Theologou; Tel. (22420) 27251.* Open daily 5pm–midnight (closed mid-November–mid-December). The restaurant takes its name from the fact that it is housed in a traditional *petrino,* or residence. It is said to be the finest place to eat on the island, and the food and the setting are both exquisite and refined. The menu features several European dishes alongside a selection of Greek specialities which are cooked to perfection. The wine cellar is filled with the best domestic varieties. Major credit cards accepted.

Taverna Ambeli €€–€€€ *Zipari, Kos; Tel. (22420) 69682.* Open April–October daily 10am–midnight, November–March daily 6pm–midnight. Family-run taverna lying to the west of Tigaki that serves delicious, freshly cooked dishes and particularly good *mezedes.* Only the freshest ingredients are used here. Wonderful, home-produced country wine (made from the vines surrounding the dining terrace and blanketing nearby fields) is served from the barrel. In winter, blazing log fires heat the interior dining room. Cash only.

Taverna Ampravis €€–€€€ *Ampravis hamlet, 1 km (1/2 mile) south of Kos Town; Tel. (22420) 25696.* Open April–October, daily 5pm–2am. With tables set in a verdant courtyard, this family-run restaurant offers some respite from the hubbub of Kos Town. Delicious Greek dishes, especially the *dolmades*, which is made in the traditional Dodecanese way with cabbage leaves. Cash only.

NISSYROS

Iy Fabrika €€–€€€ *Mandhraki.* Traditional dishes served indoors or outside in what was once a wine press. Evenings only. Music.

Taverna Irini €€–€€€ *Plaka Ilikomeni, Mandhraki.* Sought-after for its good-sized portions of fish and meat.

PATMOS

Pantelis Restaurant €–€€ *on the street parallel to the seafront, Skala; Tel. (22470) 31230.* Open May–October, daily 11am–11pm. All the Greek staples in ample portions, which assures a good local clientele along with visitors waiting to catch ferries. Tables in the street or in the spacious dining room. Cash only.

Patmian House €€€–€€€€ *off Plateia Xanthos, Hora, Patmos; Tel. (22470) 31180.* Open Easter–October, daily 7pm–midnight. The reputation of this restaurant has spread across Greece and beyond. The setting in a restored 17th-century house has been featured in numerous architectural and travel magazines, and the food matches the surroundings. Greek/Continental dishes. Cash only.

Vagelis €€€ *Main Square, Chora; Tel. (22470) 31967.* Open May–October, daily noon–1am. Popular taverna with tables in the square or on a roof terrace. Greek dishes served with care by the long-standing owners. Major credit cards.

THE EASTERN AEGEAN

LESVOS

The Galley Restaurant €€–€€€ *The Harbour, Molyvos. No phone.* Open mid-April–late October, daily 12 noon–midnight. An English-run restaurant that uses the freshest local ingredients in an innovative way. Cash only.

O Rigas €€ *next to the Theophilos Hotel, Petra; Tel. (22530) 41405.* A typical taverna serving freshly cooked dishes. Guests go into the kitchen to peruse the offerings before making their choice. An authentic experience and delicious food. From 7pm. Cash only.

CHIOS

O Morias €€–€€€ *in the town square at Mesta. No phone.* Open year-round, daily for lunch 11am–3pm and dinner 6pm–midnight.

Typical Greek taverna set in the heart of a medieval mastic village. Enjoy a leisurely lunch or hearty evening meal of traditional dishes. Cash only.

Stelios (Tou Koupelou) €€ *On the seafront, Langada.* Of all the tavernas specialising in fish that used to line the quayside of this pretty harbour, this is one of the last – and the best – still in operation. Open all year.

Theodhosiou Ouzeri € *Neorion 33, Chios Town.* The oldest ouzo bar in the town. Although it has moved to new premises it still retains a traditional atmosphere. Menu offers a wide selection of dishes. Evenings only, closed Sunday.

THE SPORADES

SKIATHOS

Taverna Asprolithos €€€–€€€€ *Odos Korai, Skiathos Town; Tel. (24270) 23110.* Open year-round, daily 7pm–1am. An elegant restaurant where service is more attentive than usual. The menu is mostly Greek, though prepared with a lighter hand and greater care, which is reflected in the price. Major credit cards.

Taverna Giorgios €€ *Trion Ierarchion Square (above the harbour), Skiathos Town. No phone.* Open April–October, daily 5pm–midnight. Set under a canvas on the cobbled street above the fishing harbour, this restaurant features barbecue meats that are cooked before your eyes. Choose whatever you think looks most appealing. Cash only.

SKOPELOS

Finikas Taverna €€–€€€ *at the top of Skopelos Town; Tel. (24240) 23247.* Open year-round, daily 6pm–midnight. Although difficult to find, this taverna is a relaxing place to eat, with views from its garden over the rooftops of Skopelos Town. Finikas often serves traditional dishes not found at most tavernas. Cash only.

INDEX